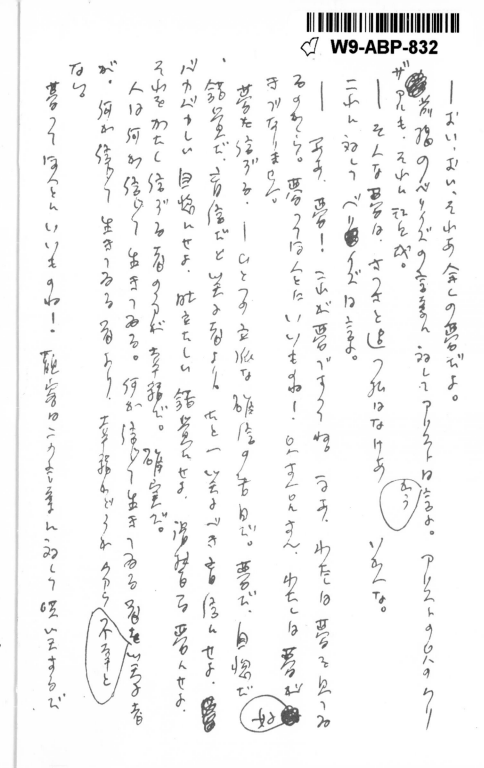

SO LOVELY A COUNTRY W...

ASIA PERSPECTIVES

WEATHERHEAD EAST ASIAN INSTITUTE · COLUMBIA UNIVERSITY

DONALD KEENE

SO LOVELY A COUNTRY WILL NEVER PERISH

WARTIME DIARIES OF JAPANESE WRITERS

COLUMBIA UNIVERSITY PRESS · NEW YORK

Columbia University Press
Publishers Since 1893
New York   Chichester, West Sussex

Library of Congress Cataloging-in-Publication Data

Keene, Donald.
    So lovely a country will never perish : wartime diaries of Japanese
writers / Donald Keene.
        p. cm.—(Asia perspectives)
    Includes bibliographical references and index.
    ISBN 978-0-231-15146-7 (cloth : alk. paper)
    ISBN 978-0-231-52272-4 (e-book)
    1. Authors, Japanese—20th century—Diaries.   2. World War, 1939–1945—
Personal narratives, Japanese.   3. World War, 1939–1945—Japan.   4. World War,
1939–1945—Literature and the war.   5. Nagai, Kafu, 1879–1959—Diaries.
6. Takami, Jun, 1907–1965—Diaries.   7. Yamada, Futaro, 1922–2001—Diaries.
I. Title.   II. Series.
    PL723.K42 2010
    940.53'520922—dc22

                                                                    2009041198

∞

Columbia University Press books are printed on permanent and durable acid-free paper.
This book is printed on paper with recycled content.
Printed in the United States of America
c 10 9 8 7 6 5 4 3 2 1

SO LOVELY A COUNTRY WILL NEVER PERISH

THIS BOOK consists mainly of selections from diaries kept by Japanese writers from late 1941 to late 1946—from the start of the Pacific War, after the bombing of Pearl Harbor, to the end of the first year of the Allied Occupation. Apart from Nagai Kafū, none of the writers represented is known abroad, but all enjoyed considerable celebrity in Japan. A few related in detail their thoughts and actions on every day of the entire period, but others, though their diaries contain entries for only a few weeks, are also valuable because they attest to the variety of reactions to the year of triumph and the following years of defeat.

Innumerable diaries by persons who were not professional writers also survive from the period. Excerpts from such diaries have been published in recent years, and some have been translated.[1] Many more were no doubt discarded or destroyed by members of the diarists' families, sure that nobody would be interested in the happenings recorded by their father, uncle, or grandfather. The surviving diaries by "unknown" Japanese tend to be repetitious because the writers usually lacked the literary skill to make their experiences distinctive, but occasionally there is a cry from the heart, and this, even if clumsily expressed, is affecting. I wish I could read all the diaries, in the hope of finding at least a few memorable passages in each, but this would be an endless task, far beyond my powers. I have chosen instead to discuss the comparatively small number of diaries kept by established authors.

My interest in diaries began during the Pacific War when for three years my main task (as a U.S. Navy translator) was to read captured documents, including the diaries of Japanese soldiers and sailors. Reading the moving descriptions of the hardships suffered by men who probably died on some atoll in the South Pacific soon after writing the last entry made me feel a closeness to the Japanese greater than any book I had read, whether scholarly or popular.

Of the diarists represented in this book, I knew Itō Sei and Takami Jun fairly well. It was largely at my recommendation that Itō spent a year at Columbia University. Takami was a familiar figure at literary gatherings. I spent perhaps an hour or so with Nagai Kafū and, years later, with Hirabayashi Taiko. I never met Yamada Fūtarō, but we were born in the same year and were linked by the same enthusiasm for French literature. I wish I had known Watanabe Kazuo, a scholar worshipped by generations of students of French literature at Tokyo University.

I have on the whole confined myself to diaries, though I have occasionally made use of newspaper and magazine articles published about the same time as the diaries were written. Yoshida Ken'ichi (1912–1977), though he was not a diarist, has been quoted because he was unique among the authors in his extraordinary fluency in English and his profound knowledge of English literature, but above all, because for forty years he was a close friend. I have not included reminiscences of the war written in later years or works of fiction.

Because my emphasis has been on individual diarists, rather than on the circumstances under which all Japanese lived at the time, I have not attempted to present a rounded picture of political or cultural developments. But I believe that the diaries, extremely varied in point of view and manner, well convey the experience of the Japanese people during a momentous period of their history.

THE MAJOR DIARISTS

Nagai Kafū (1879–1959) was a senior, celebrated writer when the Pacific War broke out. His most recent novel *Bokutō kidan* (*A Strange Tale from East of the River*) had appeared in 1937, when it was enthusiastically received by the public and praised by critics as his masterpiece. But the outbreak of war in China in the same year led the government to issue directives intended to discourage or totally prevent the publication of works (like Kafū's) that did not promote the martial resolve of the people. Would-be publishers were intimidated by such directives, and almost nothing new by Kafū, though he had been a highly popular writer, appeared during the war. This at first did not upset Kafū financially. He had inherited a considerable amount of money and continued to receive royalties from earlier works. He wrote a few stories during the war, most not published until it ended.

Kafū's chief literary activity during the war years was writing the diary he had begun in 1917. He took this diary with him (along with his bankbooks) wherever he went. Even people who knew nothing else about Kafū knew this bit of gossip and sometimes embellished it with the revelation that wherever Kafū went, he carried his entire fortune with him. He was seldom photographed except in the company of chorus girls. This reputation for eccentricity benefited him during the war by establishing him in the eyes of the police as a harmless old codger; they did not interrogate him or attempt to read his diary. Kafū was lucky: the police did not tolerate criticism of the government, and almost every page of his diary contains expressions of disgust with the military, whether sarcasm over their stupidity or annoyance because the war they started had deprived him of his favorite imported goods.

Kafū apparently considered the diary to be his most important work. Some critics concur in this judgment, praising the sharpness of his observations and the concise, classical style Kafū employed throughout; but he is more likely to be remembered for his stories evoking the old Tokyo, the city he loved even after it was almost totally destroyed.

The popular novelist Takami Jun (1907–1965) kept the most extensive diary of the war years (and later). It opens in January 1941, the day he left Tokyo on the first stage of a journey to Indonesia. When the diary was published in 1965, Takami wrote in a preface that he had never previously kept a diary because the police, never forgetting his arrest in the early 1930s as a Marxist, regularly searched his house for documents that might indicate he was secretly maintaining leftist connections. Takami was given the chance to escape surveillance when he was chosen for a mission to Bali to gather information for the government. Takami did not state the nature of his work, but he related that he came to sympathize with the people of Bali and to desire their liberation from their white colonial masters. This was one subject on which leftists and Japanese militarists could agree.

Takami returned briefly to Japan, but soon after the outbreak of war in December 1941, he was conscripted by the military and sent to Burma as a member of a team of writers and other intellectuals who, it was hoped, would strengthen ties with leaders of the conquered countries of Southeast Asia. Takami became friendly with high-ranking Burmese who expressed to him their gratitude to Japan for having liberated their country from Britain.

Takami again returned to Japan, only to be sent by the army in 1944 to China and Manchuria. He found much to interest him, but his most vivid impressions were of witnessing the harshness of the Japanese military toward the Chinese. These experiences would color his reactions to the Allied Occupation of Japan, which began in September 1945.

Takami returned from China shortly before the worst bombing of Tokyo, on March 10, 1945. Apparently he still feared the police: nowhere in his diary did he openly express antipathy for the militarism that dominated Japan. Feeling he had no choice but to cooperate, he wrote some works of which he later felt deeply ashamed. Shortly before the war ended, when it seemed likely the entire Japanese population would be mobilized, he told his wife that he was ready to die for the emperor.

Takami desperately hoped for an end to the war, even if (though he did not write this in so many words) it was in defeat. When the end came, he at first felt depression over the reality of defeat, but despair gave way to exhilaration when the Occupation forces, whose arrival he and every other Japanese had dreaded, brought the first freedom he had known.

Takami's diary affected but did not surprise me. The attitudes he expressed corresponded to my impressions of the man from his writings. The diary of Itō Sei (1905–1969), however, came as a shock. The person revealed in its pages, especially those written just after the outbreak of war, did not in the least resemble the soft-spoken, humorous, kindly man I had known. The outbreak of war in 1941 stirred an outburst of patriotism in many normally pacific Japanese, but few exulted, as Itō did, in the opportunity the war provided the Japanese to demonstrate by defeating the "Anglo-Saxon" powers that the Japanese race was the finest in the world.

Itō was a translator of English literature, a member of the group that made the first Japanese translation of *Ulysses* in the 1930s. His early works also show the marked influence of James Joyce, whom he called his "master." It is easy to imagine that the strain of translating Joyce might have inspired dislike for the "Anglo-Saxons," and Itō possibly resented the fact that, though the Japanese translated even the most difficult works of English literature, the "Anglo-Saxons" showed no interest in modern Japanese literature. But the hatred Itō displayed in his diary went beyond the frustration he may have felt as a translator; something explosive within Itō, despite his mild manner, found its outlet in the diary.

Reading the diary of Yamada Fūtarō (1922–2001) proved I was wrong in supposing that the books one reads form one's character and beliefs. He and I had read, at about the same times, the same books, yet our outlooks on the world were radically different. Yamada intensely desired a Japanese victory and refused to consider that the war might end with anything but a victory. Even after witnessing the bombing of Tokyo, he did not waver in his conviction that Japan must never surrender. He knew that prolonging the war was likely to result in countless deaths and perhaps total destruction, but he called for Japan to fight to the last man. After the defeat, he demanded revenge, a lone voice among many acclaiming the new freedom.

Yamada was an omnivorous reader and continued to read amid the bombings. His diary for 1945 reveals just how many works of European and Japanese literature he managed to read in one year.[2] As a student of medicine (the reason why he was exempted from military service), he should have too busy to read works of fiction, but his diary rarely mentions medical textbooks.

Writing in 1944 when, as he was well aware, Germany was about to crumble and the U.S. Army was approaching Manila, making it likely that all of East Asia would be at the mercy of American planes, Yamada declared, "Japan does not need moderate politicians. We need, rather, men like Robespierre, Danton, Marat, or perhaps Cromwell."[3]

THE OTHER DIARISTS

Other diarists play a smaller role in the narrative than do Takami and Yamada. It was a great disappointment to discover that the wartime diary of Tanizaki Jun'ichirō (1886–1965), the greatest writer of the period, was so uninteresting that I was seldom tempted to quote it. The diary of the lesser known journalist Kiyosawa Kiyoshi (1890–1945), by contrast, called for frequent citation because it was so frankly opposed to the military. Kiyosawa did not begin his diary until October 1942. A friend, the president of the publishing company Chūō Kōron Sha, warned him of the danger. He admitted that he was not without apprehension, but wrote, "The Greater East Asia War will decide the fate of our country. It is the duty of the writer to leave behind some sort of account of this war, for the sake of people of later times. I have begun to keep a diary of a kind I have never previously written. It is intended to serve as material for a future history of foreign relations in East Asia."[4]

Although Kiyosawa hid his diary and was careful in conversations, he heard rumors a dozen times that he was about to be arrested by the military police.[5] But he felt obliged to tell the truth, sure that nobody else, not even high-ranking officials or cabinet members, spoke the truth any more: "There is absolutely no chance in Japan to discuss politics honestly."[6]

An article in *Time* describing the Japanese army's last day on Saipan, just before the Americans took control of the island, was translated and published in the major Japanese newspapers. The account was horrifying, reporting that women and small children had jumped to their deaths from a precipice, rather than be taken prisoner by the Americans. Kiyosawa was appalled particularly by the praise the newspapers showered on the women for killing themselves and their children.[7] The correspondent of the *Yomiuri shinbun* acclaimed the mothers as "the pride of Japanese women! The finest act of the Shōwa period." In the *Asahi shinbun*, Professor Hiraizumi Kiyoshi of Tokyo University declared, "A hundred or a thousand instants of bravery emit brilliant flashes of light, an act without equal in all of history." Kiyosawa, however, concluded,

> It is my heartfelt desire that Japan progress in a sound manner. I was born in this country. I shall die in this country, and my children and grandchildren will have the same fate. I pray that our people will abandon such ideas as the belief that brute force makes a country great, and that they will awaken to the truth that only wisdom can save the country. If the "philosophy of revenge" should be the motivating power of a revival of the people, there is no hope for them.[8]

The two women whose diaries I have excerpted make a striking contrast: Princess Nashimoto Itsuko (1882–1976), who, when the war ended, expressed bitter regret that the Japanese had never given the Americans a taste of their own medicine by bombing the United States mainland, and Hirabayashi Taiko (1905–1972), who on August 15,

1945, celebrated the end of the war by joyfully removing the blackout curtains from her windows, even though all the other houses in her village remained dark.

THE DIARIES, whether detailed or fragmentary, were of the highest importance to the writers. Nagai Kafū, though he lost virtually all his possessions in the firebombing of Tokyo, saved his diary. Uchida Hyakken (1889–1971), after his house was destroyed in an air raid, took shelter in a vacant hut without conveniences; the first thing he did the next day was to bring his diary up to date. Takami Jun and Itō Sei wrote extensively every day, regardless of what other commitments they had. Tokugawa Musei (1894–1971) was dismayed to learn that his wife had sent his diaries to a safe place in the country. He feared that they might get lost on the way:

> If this diary has been permanently lost, it won't be worth my continuing it. The value of a diary is reduced if it is not complete. It isn't that I have kept a diary every single day since I was a boy. Even in the sections that describe recent years, there are many gaps. All the same, the diary is a record, with interruptions, of my life from 1929 to the present.
>
> I obviously expect and hope that my diary will in the future be read by other people. I pray that it will in some sense be of service to mankind. This prayer definitely includes the hope that those who read it will recognize me for what I was worth. However, the likelihood that my diary will be read is extremely remote. More likely, with my death the diary will become no more than meaningless scraps of paper. I foresee this, too.[9]

Few diarists intended from the start to publish their diaries. They hoped that people of the future would read them and learn what they and their time were like, but they clung to the idea of the diary as a personal and private document. Nagai Kafū was the first to discover (after the war) that it was easier to publish sections from his diary than to write a new essay or short story. Other diarists, like Takami Jun, waited for fifteen or twenty years before publishing. Still others, like Itō Sei, did not permit publication during their lifetimes. Perhaps Itō was embarrassed by his wartime fervor, though by the time of his death most people were ready to forgive him and every other diarist for their wartime effusions.

All the diaries that inspired this book were published and are familiar to scholars of the period. However, they have been used surprisingly little as source materials by those who have described the disaster of Japan's Greater East Asia War.[10]

1

MANY JAPANESE, including some who had never kept a diary, started one on December 8, 1941, the day that war broke out with Britain and America.[1] Sure that the war would rank as a major event of Japanese history, they painstakingly noted each development reported in the press, hoping that their diaries would help to preserve the events of a glorious era. Of the innumerable diaries kept throughout the country, those of persons who were or later became professional writers are probably the most interesting. The coming of the war moved many of them to intense enthusiasm, regardless of their previous political stance. Aono Suekichi (1890–1961), a leading left-wing literary critic who had been imprisoned for his views, wrote in his diary on learning of the outbreak of war that the time had come for him, as a subject of His Majesty, to render thanks to his country by offering up his life. On January 1, 1942, he wrote, "A day so pellucidly clear it makes one want to say, 'The waves of the four seas are at peace.' Heaven and Earth seem to acclaim this New Year of victories. The feeling is strong that Japan is the Land of the Gods."[2]

The doubts that many men, especially those who disliked the military leaders, had entertained about the wisdom of taking on such powerful adversaries as America and Britain were swept away in a surge of patriotism. Every fresh victory scored by the Imperial Japanese Army and Navy during the first year of the war intensified this emotion. Few diarists resisted the nationwide euphoria created by the flood of triumphs. Nagai Kafū (1879–1959) was perhaps the least moved. He wrote on December 8:

> While still in bed, I started writing the first chapter of *Fuchin* [*Sinking or Swimming*]. In the evening went to Doshūbashi. A newspaper extra reporting the commencement of hostilities between Japan and America was being hawked. On the way back home, I stopped at a Ginza restaurant. While I was eating, blackout controls went into effect, and the lights in shops along the street were gradually extinguished; but the streetcars and cars did not switch off their lights. When I boarded the Roppongi streetcar, there was, in the midst of the mob of passengers, a patriot who delivered an oration in an ear-splitting voice.[3]

Four days later, Kafū wrote,

> On the heels of the declaration of war, posters have been put up along the streets, in streetcars and restaurants, and everywhere else. They say "Slaughter them! The English and Americans are our enemies! Advance like a hundred million balls of fire!" People today have a habit of supposing that ending sentences with

da gives them force. This is a case of inept sentiments in inept language.[4]

Kafū continued throughout the war to express disdain for each manifestation of patriotism he observed. His diary describes the military in terms that grew ever harsher as the war went on. He was especially irritated by the crudity of patriotic slogans.

The years Kafū had spent in America and France and his special devotion to French literature may have made him less susceptible to propaganda than most Japanese intellectuals. But, in fact, there was surprisingly little relation between a writer's experiences abroad and his approval or disapproval of the war. Takamura Kōtarō (1883–1956), one of the most impassioned supporters of the war, had studied sculpture in both the United States and France, but the mood of his poem "Jūnigatsu yōka," celebrating the attack on Pearl Harbor, has none of Kafū's haughty indifference. It opens

Remember December eighth!
On this day the history of the world was changed.
The Anglo-Saxon powers
On this day were driven back on East Asian land and sea,
It was their *Japan* that drove them back,
A tiny country in the Eastern Sea,
Nippon, the Land of the Gods
Ruled over by a living god.[5]

Takamura's hostility to the "Anglo-Saxons" has been traced to the racial discrimination he encountered while studying in New York. He resented being called a "Jap" and hearing his country referred to as Japan instead of Nippon. Such experiences may explain Takamura's resentment, though not the vehemence.

The poet Noguchi Yonejirō (1875–1947), unlike Takamura, had little cause for complaint about the treatment he had received abroad. He traveled to America when he was eighteen and met the then well-known poet Joaquin Miller, who not only persuaded him to become a poet but introduced him to the circle of San Francisco poets. Before long, Noguchi, under the name Yone Noguchi, was taken up by the Imagists, who found his charming poems written in English strikingly close to their own. Noguchi also wrote fiction in English, including *Letters of a Japanese Parlor-Maid* (1906). He married an American[6] and had numerous American and British friends. His poems in Japanese, less accomplished than those in English, struck readers as being somehow foreign. His best-known collection of poetry in Japanese, published in 1921, was called *Poems by a Man with Dual Nationality*. Yet this man of two nationalities would express unusual hostility to the West in the poems he composed during the war. One poem, published in 1944, bears the title "Slaughter Them! The Americans and British Are Our Enemies." It opens

> The town overflows with the cry,
> "Slaughter them! The Americans and British are our enemies."
> I too shout it. I shout till my voice is hoarse. I shout in tears.
> These were the countries that nurtured me for twelve years when
> I was young.
> Even an act of ingratitude cannot be measured against a nation's
> fate;
> The ties of the past are a dream.
> America and England in the old days were for me countries of
> justice:
> America was the country of Whitman,
> England the country of Browning;
> But now they are dissolute countries fallen into the pit of wealth,
> Immoral countries, craving after unpardonable dreams.[7]

The poem goes on to suggest that if his old friends in America and England were to meet him now, they would probably say, "This is a war between country and country. Our friendship is too sacred to be destroyed." In the last line of the poem, Noguchi gave his reply to their plea: "We'll show you how decisively we slaughter you and your friendship."

Blame for starting the war, regardless of which side fired the first shots, was placed by the poets on dissolute, materialistic countries like Britain and America that had fallen into "a pit of wealth." The poet Kawada Jun (1882–1956) composed a tanka asserting that on December 8 the English and Americans had revealed their true ferocity:

tsui ni sono	At last, they have
kamen nugisute	Discarded their masks
kiba wo muku	And bared their fangs:
igirisu yakko	The English villains,
amerika yakko	The American villains.[8]

It is rather strange that the English and Americans, rather than the Japanese, were accused of starting the war; patriotism took precedence over facts.

Novelists revealed sentiments that were quite as bellicose as those of the poets Takamura and Noguchi. Itō Sei (1905–1969), in both his diary and his essays, expressed delight over the commencement of the war and the anticipated destruction of the Anglo-Saxons, though his first reactions on learning of the attack on Pearl Harbor were surprisingly moderate. He noted in his diary that nobody he saw on the streets or in the buses seemed to be concerned about the war; pedestrians even looked rather glum. But Itō was exhilarated by news that American warships had been sunk during the raid on Pearl Harbor: "The Japanese way of doing things recalls the Russo-Japanese War. It is wonderful."[9] Itō was apparently referring to the Japanese attack without prior declaration of war on Russian warships in 1904. The surprise assaults that had caught the enemy unawares at Port Arthur and, thirty-seven years later, at Pearl Harbor were certainly effective, but they aroused outrage abroad over what were deemed violations of international conventions on the conduct of war.

Itō felt no need to justify his jubilation, though we might expect that his close connections with the English language, as both a teacher and a translator, would have given him pause. On December 8, he wrote in his diary,

Our destiny is such that we cannot realize our qualifications as first-class people of the world unless we have fought with the top-ranking white men.

I have come to understand for the first time as a reality—and with boundless affection—the meaning of each and every aspect of Japan and the Japanese.

An article Itō published on December 9 was even more outspoken:

Yesterday Japan's war with Britain and America began. We do not know how long this war, the greatest in the history of the Yamato race, will last. . . .

When I saw the headline "Great, Death-Defying Air Attack on Pearl Harbor in Hawaii," my whole body became rigid and my eyes danced so much I couldn't read. . . .

Then, while leaning against the white wall of the basement, I had a feeling of awakening as if water had suddenly been poured over my entire body. Yes, the vindication of our sense of superiority of the race is driving us forward. This is an absolute act, I thought. This war is not an extension of politics or another face of politics. It is a war we had to fight at some stage in order for us to believe firmly, from the depths of our hearts, that the Yamato race is the most superior on the globe.

I, like most other Japanese intellectuals, began the study of English at the age of thirteen, and it brought me in contact with the world. This, of course, was because the races who use English possess the finest culture, the greatest strength and riches of any country in the world. In this sense, up to now they had been the supreme rulers of the world. This awareness had seeped into our guts. And as long as such an awareness was within us, it could not but prevent us from being convinced that the Yamato race was the most superior in the world. . . .

I believe that Japanese intellectuals, as members of the Yamato race, are sure that fighting this war to the finish is absolutely indispensable. We are the so-called "yellow race." We are fighting

to determine the superiority of a race that has been discrimi-
nated against. Our war is not the same as Germany's. Their war is
a struggle among similar countries for advantage. Our war is a
struggle for a predestined confidence.[10]

In these writings, Itō repeatedly used the word *minzoku* (race) not in
speaking of the major segment of humanity that includes not only
Japanese but Chinese, Koreans, and other Asians, but in referring specifically to the Yamato race: the Japanese.[11] Itō was told on December
16 that he should not use the words "yellow" and "white" when writing
about the antagonists and was directed to say instead "the Anglo-
Saxons" or "Britain and America."[12] It is not clear who issued this directive. Perhaps the military, more conscious than Itō that Japan was the
ally of two "white" countries, Germany and Italy, were anxious not to
give Japan's war the character of a struggle between races. Later on,
when the liberation of Greater East Asia was officially proclaimed as
the ultimate goal of the war, the objections to expressing prejudices
against non-Asians were forgotten.

Itō predicted that after the war ended, there would be a splendid
flowering of literature and that it would be quite different from the literature of the early Shōwa period. He was right in this prediction, but
he did not foresee the nature of the changes that occurred. Nor could
he have foreseen that the greatest fame he would enjoy in his lifetime
was (in the postwar years) as the translator of *Lady Chatterley's Lover*,
a novel by an Anglo-Saxon.

Itō had a shock on December 12, as he recorded in his diary. On that
day, Takasu Yoshijirō (1888–1948), a senior teacher at the school where
Itō taught, denounced liberalism in literature. This made Itō think that
"it would be necessary, with a view to the future of ten or twenty years
from now, to take this opportunity to reconstruct the content of my
ideology. I must, in my own way, quickly make my awareness as a Japanese more systematic."[13]

Itō, whose struggles with the English language had culminated in
the translation of James Joyce's *Ulysses*, seems to have realized at this
point that he would have to give up the liberalism implicit in translating

such works, but he could not do it immediately. He needed the income from translations and had promised a publisher to translate D. H. Lawrence's *Mexican Morning*. He did not feel that translating a work by an enemy author constituted proof that he recognized the writer's superiority.

As the war progressed, Itō lost some of the fire of his convictions about the Yamato race. It is true that he took to reading the *Kojiki* (*Record of Ancient Matters*, 712), the bible of Shintoism, and considered comparing it with accounts of the Greater East Asia War, but he reported in his diary entry for March 3, 1942: "On looking through this month's literary magazines and coterie magazines, it is apparent that the hot-headed *Nippon shugi* [Japanism] of the beginning of the war has been relaxed, and writers are basing their writings on a kind of literary spirit of humanism."[14] But Itō never doubted the goals of the war or the certainty of a Japanese victory. He wrote on March 12: "I opened a map of the world and was astonished at the extent of the conquests by the Japanese. India may be more difficult to take if it resists as strongly as China, but Australia won't be difficult once we occupy the cities on the periphery."[15]

Other Japanese who had been deeply devoted to European literature and made it their profession seemed willing and even happy to shed this knowledge once war broke out. Yoshida Ken'ichi (1912–1977), who spoke and wrote English faultlessly and whose most important works (published after the war) were studies of English literature, wrote in December 1941:

> Ever since December eighth we have been living with completely changed ideas. Things that remain the same as before no longer seem the same because a new awareness unquestionably controls our minds and hearts as an undeniable truth. I realize this is exactly what for long months and years we had been awaiting. But who could have predicted this time would arrive today? We lacked even the conviction to say that this day should come, in the form it has taken. . . .

It needs hardly be said that the war is just beginning. But it definitely has begun, and that is the historical significance of the day. We must be ready for the fighting that will ensue. But even as we bask in this glory, what can we do apart from revitalizing our resolve? It is a vital resolve whose meaning we should ponder moment by moment.

We are not letting ourselves get carried away. While this un-wavering emotion persists, everything seems fresh and new. We need not fear even air attacks. The sky of our thought has been cleared of England and America.[16]

The image of the sky being cleared of the oppressive clouds of En-glish and American superiority occurs in writings by other men. Saitō Ryū (1879–1953), a former general turned poet, wrote this tanka:

beiei wo	The time has come
hōmuru toki kite	To slaughter America and England.
ana sugashi	Ah, how refreshing!
shiten ichiji ni	The clouds in the four heavens
kumo harenikeri	Have simultaneously cleared.[17]

When protracted negotiations with the United States were broken off and the Japanese navy initiated the war by bombing Pearl Harbor, a feeling of refreshment was commonly expressed by those who believed that anything was better than unremitting tension. This was perhaps to be expected in someone of General Saitō's background, but the attitude is surprising in Yoshida, a scholar of English literature.

The diarists, especially the few who opposed the war or merely doubted its advisability, were aware that intellectuals were under the surveillance of the police and were at pains to avoid expressing criti-cism of the government in their diaries. Takami Jun (1907–1965), who kept an extremely detailed diary of the war years (some three thousand pages), described the visit on January 7, 1945, of a friend who confessed that he wanted to keep a diary, but was afraid of the consequences:

there was no telling when and for what reason one's house might be searched, and a diary might be used as a pretext for making an arrest. Takami evidently thought that keeping a diary was worth the risk.[18]

Kiyosawa Kiyoshi (1890–1945), a journalist whose diary is shot through with bitter criticism of the war, was warned by his publisher (some of whose publications had just been carried off by the police as suspicious) of the danger of keeping a diary. Kiyosawa wrote, "I am not without apprehension when I write this diary."[19]

Despite the danger, some authors resolutely wrote entries every day. Takami Jun's diary took precedence over other obligations, and when (as occasionally happened) he neglected the diary for a day or two, he apologized. Nagai Kafū, who lost three houses to wartime bombing, managed to save his diary by carrying it with him in a satchel at all times. Itō Sei wrote on December 17, 1944:

> I have come to realize that this diary, which I began to write as a mere chronicle, is now the most important work of my life. In it I have set down truthfully, for the benefit of people of the future, the beauty of the Japanese race, their suffering, the manner in which they fought, the different aspects of their lives. I shall probably soon be sent to the battlefield, but until that day comes, I will continue writing.[20]

Writing a diary as detailed as Takami's must have greatly interfered with his normal literary production. A few writers kept diaries with the intention of eventually converting them into salable manuscripts, but Takami and Kafū initially had no thought of publishing their diaries. Only after the war did they publish what some critics subsequently acclaimed as their finest works.

The great majority of wartime diaries were, of course, kept not by writers or other intellectuals but by quite ordinary Japanese, both civilian and military. Keeping a diary was a tradition in Japan that dated back to the tenth century, and Japanese, even in uneventful times, felt it necessary to preserve in writing quite ordinary experiences, whether as aide-mémoires for their old age or as guides for the edification of their children. Every soldier and sailor was issued a diary at the New Year. American servicemen were forbidden to keep diaries, for fear that they might contain information of use to the enemy, but Japanese soldiers and sailors were encouraged by their superiors to keep diaries, perhaps so they could be inspected from time to time in order to make sure that the diarists were unshaken in their support of the "holy war."

During the war, writers commonly predicted each New Year's Day that this year (whichever it was) would determine the fate of Japan. The year 1945 undoubtedly did precisely that. On January 1, 1945, Yamada Fūtarō (1922–2001), a medical student at the time,[21] wrote in his diary,

A fateful year has begun. The life or death of Japan hangs on this one year. I pray either to live for my country or to die for it.

Three air raids by B-29s last night—at ten, midnight, and five in the morning. Instead of the sound of temple bells ringing out the old year, there were the weird noises of interceptor guns, and in place of purifying fire on the altars, there was the color of conflagrations in the sky. I heard that bombs were dropped in the area of Kuramae in Asakusa. Close to a thousand houses burned in one night.[22]

The first air raid on Japan had taken place on April 18, 1942, when sixteen medium-range bombers under the command of Major General James Doolittle dropped bombs on what the United States officially described as military targets in Tokyo, though the photographs of their accomplishments prove only that they sank a small fishing boat. The planes took off from an aircraft carrier, but, because they were too heavy to land on the carrier deck, once they completed their mission they headed for safety in China. This was no more than a token raid, intended more to boost American morale than to cause damage to targets in Tokyo. It nevertheless caused uneasiness among the Japanese. The day after Doolittle's raid, Itō Sei put up blackout curtains and decided that he would wear Western clothes instead of a kimono, in order to enjoy greater mobility.[23] Nagai Kafū wrote in his diary,

April 18. In the evening I went to Kinbei [a drinking place] and learned for the first time that American airplanes had attacked Tokyo this afternoon and had dropped bombs. People said fires were started in the areas of Waseda, Shimo Meguro, Mikawajima, and Asakusa Tanaka-chō. The Kabuki Theater has been closed since noon. Shows in Asakusa shut down at six, and there was nothing open at night. The newspapers did not publish an extra.

April 19.

Ever since the attack by American planes, there seems to be general anxiety. After a nap, I went to Kinbei and listened to what people were saying. A factory on the Ōimachi railway line was destroyed by fire, and two or three hundred men and women who worked there were killed or injured. In the Imado section of Asakusa, people were wounded by fragments of a falling anti-aircraft shell. A factory in the Komatsugawa section was hit by a bomb and burned. The newspapers and radio are maintaining their usual silence, and for this reason there are all kinds of rumors. It is not possible to get a definite report.[24]

A scarcity of reliable information would characterize the war from this early stage. Much of what Kafū reported was no more than rumors. Although reports from Japanese correspondents stationed in Sweden, Portugal, and other neutral countries kept readers informed even about events unfavorable to the Axis, damage incurred within Japan or in places abroad occupied by Japanese troops either was not reported or was minimized. Newspaper accounts of imaginary victories over the American fleet or over American troops who had gone ashore on some Pacific island brought comfort and joy; few, even among the intellectuals, openly wondered how the Americans could continue to fight even after suffering the staggering losses reported in the press.

The newspapers assured the Japanese that their air defenses were the best in the world, and when enemy bombs managed to fall on Japanese cities despite the vaunted defenses, the buildings hit by American bombers were always identified as schools and hospitals. The public's trust in such communiqués declined once the Americans seized air control over the home islands. It is estimated that by the end of 1944, after the loss of Leyte in the Philippines and the start of massive air raids on Tokyo, one-third of the Japanese had begun to doubt the likelihood of a Japanese victory.[25]

Because of the controls exerted on speech and the press, rumors took the place of information, and the prevalence of rumors has even been interpreted as a form of resistance to the official reports and to the militarists. It usually did not take long for the rumors to be discredited and forgotten, but false rumors were rejected only to be replaced by new rumors, equally plausible if equally unfounded. Once in a while, a rumor came true. On January 16, 1945, Nagai Kafū heard that the war would end with a Japanese defeat in August of that year.[26] But this was a rare coincidence: countless unsubstantiated rumors circulated not only about the progress of the war or the places on the coast where American troops were most likely to land, but about food rationing, forced evacuation, and every other source of worry and fear that beset the Japanese in 1945.

It was usually impossible to trace rumors back to the person who had originated them. Perhaps the ultimate motivation for the creation of a rumor was a man's desire to acquire importance in his community by posing as someone who had access to information not available to other people and was therefore worthy of respect.[27]

The first major air attack on Tokyo occurred on November 1, 1944. American bombers, which had taken off from bases on the recently conquered islands of Saipan and Tinian, were met by Japanese fighters that arrived too late to shoot down any of the invaders. Japanese anti-aircraft fire also failed to hit a single plane. This should have disillusioned Japanese who had believed official claims that the air defenses were impenetrable, but diarists hardly ever expressed anger that Japanese fighters were failing to protect Tokyo from American bombs. They seem to have tacitly recognized that Japanese planes were no match for American bombers. The B-29s were given affectionate names like *Pōsuke* and *Puchan*,[28] and the diarists not infrequently commented on the beauty of the huge planes flying in formation. Occasionally those watching the sky had the consolation of seeing an American bomber drop in flames.

Full-scale air attacks began on November 24, 1944. Unno Jūza (1897–1949), a well-known writer of science fiction, never wavered in his confidence that Japan would win the war, but he congratulated himself in his diary on having had the foresight to build a large air-raid shelter in January 1941.[29] He and his family would make good use of the shelter in 1945.

American raids become frequent and reached a high level of intensity after the Americans captured Iwo Jima in March 1945, providing them with a base close enough to the main islands of Japan for planes to drop bombs on them and return without refueling. The virtually unopposed bombers managed to destroy large areas of the major cities, but most Japanese remained confident of eventual victory.

Yamada Fūtarō contrasted the nature of this confidence among the Japanese with that of people in enemy countries. Unlike America, which relied on its wealth and strength; or China, which depended on its great size; or Britain, which counted on its tradition of invincibility, Japan had nothing to sustain itself but a belief in *Yamato-damashii*, the spirit of Japan. He likened the Japanese at this stage of the war to sleepwalkers or victims of a possession who, not conscious of what they were doing, were supporting an exhausted Japan. He related conversations he had heard in the public baths, a traditional place for the exchange of gossip:

In 1942 conversation was mainly about the war. In 1943 talk about factories and food shortages took first place. In 1944 it was the black market and, toward the end of that year, the air raids. Now, no matter how devastating a raid people may have suffered, nobody says a word about it. People in the bath silently stare at the ceiling in exhaustion. Their expression is not especially one of fear or weariness with the war. They seem to be aware that it is the fate of anyone born in this country to fight, to fight, to fight to the end. . . . From the women's bath on the other side of the partition, one used to hear chattering and laughter, voices calling and children bawling, noisy as frogs on a June night in the country- side. But now there is only a silence like death. The women are also exhausted. No, the women are the ones who are totally exhausted.[30]

Yamada wrote on January 6, 1945:

In the past, at the beginning of the year, every one of our people had hopes of some kind. They made resolutions: This year I will do that work. This year I will strengthen my body. I will not lose my temper. And so on. Even if people failed to live up to their resolutions, making them was one of the pleasures of the New Year. This year there cannot be even one person who has made resolutions.[31]

There is no trace in Yamada's entry for New Year's Day or in any other diary written in 1945 of the optimism about the war recorded by diarists at the start of the three previous years. Despite the rationing and the scarcity of food, people had managed to maintain until 1944 a semblance of the traditional New Year festivities. Little girls, dressed in bright kimonos with trailing sleeves, had played the traditional game of battledore and shuttlecock. But in 1945, as Yamada observed, the streets were empty, and the only sound was the flapping of flags in the wind.

On January 3, Yamada went to see a section of the city where three hundred houses had been destroyed in an air raid on New Year's Eve:

The area was cordoned off, but it was so extensive that I was able to take in the whole, horrible scene. What filthy remains are left when houses where human beings have lived are destroyed! Galvanized-iron sheeting, burned stones, unburned wooden posts, furniture. Here and there straw matting spread out on the ground, and groups of victims of the raid trying to restore some order. Signs are pasted everywhere, giving addresses to which victims have moved. A smell of smoldering fires. The tatami and furniture that people managed to drag from their houses evoke, more than the houses that were completely gutted, the confusion of that night. I could see clearly the pale, tense faces, the wide-staring eyes, the mouths uttering inarticulate screams.[32]

Despite the later, intense bombing and despite even the atomic bomb, Yamada never wavered in his support for the war. When he heard the emperor's broadcast announcing that Japan had accepted the Allies' terms for surrender, he experienced not relief but bitter disappointment.

Kiyosawa Kiyoshi found hope in the likelihood that the Japanese would come to hate war. He wrote in his diary,

The Japanese people are experiencing war for the first time. For many years we have heard praise of war as the mother of culture and of wars that lasted a hundred years. I was persecuted for my pacifism. Did they think war is such a picnic? Now people know what it is like. All the same, I wonder if they really will be chastened by the war. The result may be the opposite. First of all, they think that war was inevitable. Second, they are intoxicated with the heroism of war. Third, they have no knowledge of international affairs. Their ignorance is astonishing.

A feeling of hatred of war will arise in time. In the meanwhile, we must provide correct education. The raising of the position of women in society is also necessary.[33]

Some never lost their enthusiasm for the holy war. Tokutomi Sohō (1863–1957), a veteran journalist and historian, worshipped the emperor as a god, but nevertheless rebuked him for ending the war. He was sure that if the emperor had taken personal command of the troops defending Japan, the spirits of his divine ancestors would have helped him repel any enemy that dared to set foot on Japanese soil. Tokutomi, probably the most conspicuous warmonger, not only kept up a stream of pro-war articles during the war but continued to write them after the defeat, though they were not published for many years.

Kiyosawa Kiyoshi, in his diary entry for January 2, 1945, quoted an article by Tokutomi, "Ichioku eiyū tare!" (Become One Hundred Million Heroes!) in the *Mainichi shinbun*. In this article, Tokutomi regretted that his meager strength had been insufficient to awaken the Japanese people. He looked forward to the dropping of bombs in the middle of Tokyo; that was the only thing that could stir up the people. Kiyosawa commented, "Has anyone ever said anything so irresponsible? Tokutomi, though he himself is responsible for starting the war, wants to make the people bear the guilt."[34]

Many Japanese wept when the war finally ended, finding it an unmitigated disaster: for the first time in its long history, Japan had been defeated. There were exceptions. Watanabe Kazuo (1901–1975), a professor at Tokyo University, wrote his diary for 1945 in French in order to prevent the police from reading his comments on the war. On August 18, three days after the emperor announced the Japanese surrender in a radio broadcast, Watanabe wrote in his diary, "At last I can write my native language again." The wartime nightmare had at last ended. There would be life-and-death problems for the Japanese to face at a time when food was scarce and unemployment was prevalent, but the worst was over.

THE REACTION of most Japanese on learning of the attack on Pearl Harbor and the declaration of war with America and Britain was exultation; this was as true of the intellectuals as of the poorly educated.[1] The festive mood was maintained through most of the first year of the war as Japanese armed forces occupied with incredible rapidity the Philippines, Hong Kong, Indochina, Burma, Malaysia, and Indonesia as well as clusters of islands in the southern and western Pacific. Australia was threatened, and Japanese forces seized two American islands (Attu and Kiska) in the northern Pacific.

The Japanese encountered resistance, notably on the Bataan Peninsula in the Philippines, but their advance was unchecked. They derided enemy commanders for their readiness to surrender in order to save their men and themselves from slaughter, sure that if they themselves had had the supply of matériel of the Americans on Bataan, they would have fought to the last soldier. The American reluctance to sustain heavy casualties represented in the eyes of Japanese a weakness that could be exploited.[2]

The widely reproduced photograph of General Yamashita Tomoyuki demanding that Lieutenant General Arthur Percival, the commander of British forces in Singapore, answer yes or no to his ultimatum of surrender caused no embarrassment even among Western-trained Japanese intellectuals; it was acclaimed instead as unmistakable proof that the Japanese, after a century of deference to the West, now held the upper hand. The photograph also served as an indication that the Japanese had no intention of observing the courtesy with which they had treated defeated enemy generals during the Sino-Japanese War and the Russo-Japanese War.[3] Colonel Odajima Kaoru said of the treatment of prisoners of war, "At the time of the Russo-Japanese War we worshipped the West, but now we are doing things in the Japanese way."[4]

The justification originally given by the Japanese for starting the war was that the ABCD powers (America, Britain, China, and the Dutch) were attempting to strangle Japan by cutting off needed raw materials. The emperor's rescript mentioned "self-existence" and "self-protection" as the aim of his nation's declaration of war. At this early stage of the war, the liberation of colonized Asia, later proclaimed as the supreme objective of the Japanese war effort, was not cited.

The Americans, not eager for a war, had hoped to preserve peace, but the terms offered by Secretary of State Cordell Hull required the Japanese to cease their support for the government they had established in China and to withdraw from French Indochina. It was inconceivable that Japan would accept these terms.

Once the war had begun, mass enthusiasm silenced possible objections. Some Japanese would insist in later years that they had known all along that Japan could not win a war with the United States and had therefore always opposed it. But during the war, extremely few expressed pessimism about the outcome, even to intimate friends or to their diaries. Not until Japan had suffered severe defeats, especially at Saipan, were voices heard warning of disaster, and even then were muted, for fear of being overheard by the feared military police.

The battle for Guadalcanal, which lasted from August 1942 to February 1943, marked the first attempt of the Americans to wrest back territory occupied by the Japanese during the first year of the war. The fighting was fierce. So many Japanese died, not only from American bullets but from hunger, that the diaries of Japanese soldiers often referred to the island as Gatō—Island of Starvation. I read these diaries, picked up on the battlefield or plucked from the sea, a few weeks later at a naval office in Pearl Harbor. Reading diaries filled with the thoughts of men suffering from hunger and disease convinced me that those who professed to understand the Japanese psychology were grossly mistaken when they said that the Japanese were fanatics devoid of normal human frailty.

The outcome of the fighting on Guadalcanal was by no means clearcut. The Japanese navy was victorious in all four sea battles fought in the area, but the cost was so high that (at least in retrospect) Guadalcanal may have been the turning point of the war.[5] However, the Japanese troops on the island were not annihilated; the high command, finally abandoning hope of driving the Americans from Guadalcanal, withdrew the surviving soldiers. Surrender was not considered.

The battle for Guadalcanal figures in diaries written by intellectuals in Japan mainly in terms of the elation aroused by news of the sinking of American and Australian ships. Little grief was expressed in these diaries for the Japanese soldiers who had lost their lives on a distant island, the diarists instead paying tribute to those who in death had became gods.

As long as Japan, despite the setback at Guadalcanal, still seemed to be winning the war, the Japanese high command did not find it necessary to conceal the number of casualties or to distort the results of the fighting. But before long, the official communiqués became unreliable, exaggerating or even inventing enemy losses and minimizing their own. Rumors filled in what the communiqués failed to reveal. Itō Sei wrote in his diary,

Last night I heard a true story. It came from the Investigation Section of the South Manchurian Railway. The report states that ten thousand of our marines on Guadalcanal were massacred. Later on, two of three ships in a convoy carrying reinforcements were sunk. One ship managed to reach shore, but the men have since been engaged in a desperate battle and are barely managing to hold the beachhead where they landed. This is top secret. I won't tell anyone.[6]

Nagai Kafū's diary does not allude to Guadalcanal. Fighting over an island in the South Pacific was of less concern to him than were the sinister plainclothes military police he noticed in his neighborhood; he guessed that they were plotting to confiscate his house. He also reported the shockingly high cost of commodities of great importance to him, such as Johnny Walker whiskey. Takami Jun did not mention Guadalcanal, though he was the most assiduous of the wartime diarists. Takami was in Burma, serving in a "Pen Unit," the name given to the delegations of writers sent abroad by the military as ambassadors of Japanese culture.

The next campaign, the battle for Attu in the Aleutian Islands, evoked much greater reactions from writers. On May 29, 1943, Itō, having read a dispatch from Attu indicating that the Americans were closing in on the Japanese garrison, wrote in alarm,

How is the Japanese Army doing on Attu? This is the season of "white nights." Our men will be subjected to gunfire and bombing almost twenty hours a day. Have they got enough ammunition? What about food? Are they able to treat the wounded? Is it because the soldiers on Attu are from Hokkaidō that this battle worries me more than any previous one?[7] Will it be possible for them to withdraw, if that is decided?

Two days later, he wrote,

Our forces on Attu have been wiped out. The 2000 and some hundreds more of our men were surrounded by 20,000 of the enemy and in the end were destroyed. On the night of the 29th, the wounded and ill committed suicide. More than a hundred of the survivors made a final charge under the command of Colonel Yamazaki [Yasuyo] and perished. . . . I don't know of any more tragic event. What can one say? It has finally come to this. The war has at last shown its true face nakedly. I feel as if I have just wakened from sleep. The fighting was even more intense than at Nomonhan or Guadalcanal.[8] There was nothing like it in the Russo-Japanese War either.

When I think that the peaceful life we lead at home is sustained by those at the front, the stillness of each day seems like a shimmering of haze. Even in the sight of people walking, streetcars running, the flourishing of young leaves can make us feel more deeply the taste of being alive and living a peaceful existence.

I wonder if the truth of such sad news will not rouse up our people? We have been too victorious, from Hawaii to Malaya, the Dutch East Indies, Burma, and the Philippines. That is why, even when the authorities repeatedly warned that the battle for the Solomons was decisive and reiterated its importance, the possibility that Japan might actually lose the war never entered the heads of the public. The battle for Attu ended in defeat and annihilation, and we are living with this defeat permeating our minds. This has made the people aware of the reality of the danger. . . . We have come at last to feel that the homeland is exposed to danger from the enemy. This no doubt will be the shape of the Greater East Asia War from this time on.[9]

A few days later, Itō read in the *Asahi shinbun* a dispatch from a Dōmei Agency reporter in Buenos Aires that gave the American version of the battle for Attu. He commented, "What a beautiful single thread of action connects the events! No sooner had the wounded committed suicide than the soldiers of Attu charged and were all killed. This is not a made-up story. It is a fact. It is a truth demonstrated by the dead soldiers' flesh. Attu will probably be the model for the Japanese Army in future warfare."[10]

Attu did indeed become a model. After the sick and wounded had been disposed of, not by their own hands (as official reports stated) but by grenades that other Japanese troops tossed into the hospital tents, the remaining soldiers made a desperate charge that ended the battle for Attu. This pattern would be repeated on other islands. The Americans referred to such charges as "banzai charges" because the Japanese screamed "Banzai!" as they rushed toward death. Back in Japan, Takami Jun wrote in his diary on May 31: "Today I learned of the *gyokusai* of our entire garrison on Attu. I felt a burning sensation in my chest."[11]

The term *gyokusai* (literally, "jewel-breaking") signified (in highly compressed language) that it was better to perish like a broken jewel than to remain whole like a worthless tile. Soldiers were inculcated with the belief that it had been a Japanese tradition ever since ancient times for fighting men to choose death rather than suffer the unforgivable disgrace of being taken prisoner.

On Attu the final, headlong attack on American positions was suicidal in intent, but the Americans, not expecting it, were very nearly swept into the sea. They eventually prevailed, and the bleak tundra of Attu was littered with the bodies of Japanese soldiers, some of whom had committed suicide by pressing hand grenades to their chests.

The *gyokusai* on Attu, the first of the war, gave the island its fame. Many poems were composed to celebrate the heroism of the Japanese defenders. The poet Maekawa Samio (1903–1990) published tanka sequences dedicated to the loyal dead of Attu, the members of the Yamazaki Force. The emphasis in these poems is not on the bravery of the soldiers, or on how they served their country, but on their deaths:

amazutau	On a northern island
hikari mo usuki	Where even the light that fills
kita no shima ni	The heavens is pale:
kami no mikusa no	Two thousand of an army
nisen shinashinu	Of gods have died in battle.

hitori dani	We shall remember
ikinokoraji to	For all ages to come
morotomo ni	How they died together,
uchitaeshi wo zo	Resolved that not even
towa ni shinuban[12]	One man would be left alive.

Haiku poets also composed poems about Attu. A haiku by Katō Shūson (1905–1993) bears the title "No Response from Attu." When an attempt was made to communicate with the Attu garrison, there was no reply; all the soldiers were dead:

kotae nashi	There is no response:
yuri no kafun wa	Pollen of the lilies
hanabira ni	Falls on the petals.

An unusual prose poem describing the battle for Attu was written by a leading Indonesian poet, Chairil Anwar (1922–1949). He sent to Ida, his girlfriend, a eulogy of Colonel Yamazaki Yasuyo, the commander of Japanese forces on Attu, who died with his men in the final charge:

> Colonel Jamasaki, Ida! A brave warrior from Attu! Ah, be in harmony with this noble spirit. The personification of the ideal! Observe, my darling, the service given to his Homeland, ever more fervently, by Tennō Heika [His Majesty, the Emperor], the sentiments reaching higher and higher—and I think most of them must be included in that life energy which flares up fantastically until it is concluded by death.[13]

Anwar's prose poem indicates that the Japanese had successfully transmitted to some Indonesians their worship not only of the Attu *gyokusai* but of the emperor.

Not every Japanese was overcome with admiration for the *gyokusai*. Nagai Kafū's diary entry for June 1, 1943, contains a passage titled "Gaidanroku" (Record of Street Conversations):

At a certain moment, Admiral Yamamoto died in battle in the South Pacific. Next, a group of patriots declared with respect to the Japanese soldiers who had landed on a lonely island in the northern sea and died there, that they were putting into practice the teachings of Lord Kusunoki.[14] ... In general, the rise or fall of a country is not determined by any one-time victory or defeat or by the life or death of a commanding officer. If, having been defeated in battle, a general kills himself, this is an action based on desperation, and is nothing but an act of individual self-satisfaction. If, for the sake of his own reputation and some momentary emotion, a leader sacrifices innocent soldiers, with no consideration for them, this must be called an extreme case of egoism.[15]

Kafū was convinced that military glory did not justify the loss of soldiers' lives. This, of course, was quite the opposite of what Japanese militarists asserted. Two days later, Kafū, who seems to have dismissed the defeat at Attu as being of no importance, complained about the militarists in a more typical manner:

June 3. Recently I have been unable to fall asleep as soon as my head touches the pillow. Usually I read until the break of day, and only then am I able to sleep. The number of foreign books on my shelves that I have yet to read has gradually diminished. There is now only one bottle left of the wine I have been hoarding along with the foreign books. I have only five or six cakes left of English soap, and very little Lipton tea. How long will the evil practices of *sakoku* and *jōi* continue?[16]

The battle for Attu, so crucial to the Japanese, was by no means of equal interest to Americans. The war in Europe—in particular, the victory of the Russians at Stalingrad and the landing of Allied troops in Sicily—was of far greater immediacy. I recall hearing newspaper reporters, sent to cover the operation at Attu, complaining of their bad luck in having to write about the grade-B war in the Pacific instead of the grade-A war in Europe. But the Japanese did not forget Attu, and even after they had lost more important bases to the Americans, they repeated the vow to take back this miserable, cold, foggy island at the end of the world.[17]

On June 17, Prime Minister Tōjō Hideki (1884–1948) delivered a speech in which he mourned the loss of Attu. As Itō Sei noted in his diary, Tōjō did not once mention Australia, though he had predicted the capture of Australia in every speech he had delivered while serving as minister of the army. The tone of the speech seems to suggest that a shift had occurred from buoyant confidence in the boundless expansion of Japanese power to an emphasis on a more specific objective, the realization of Daitōa—Greater East Asia.

The concept of Greater East Asia is usually traced back to 1940. In that year, Foreign Minister Arita Hachirō (1884–1965) proposed a union of the nations of East Asia under the guidance of Japan. His successor, Matsuoka Yōsuke (1886–1946), later that year gave a speech in which he spoke of the Greater East Asia Co-Prosperity Sphere, and this phrase was elevated into an ideal, to be evoked through the war. The Daitōa-shō (Greater East Asia Ministry) was established by the cabinet of Prime Minister Tōjō at the end of 1942 to deal with affairs concerning Japan and the various countries of the region.

The governments set up by the Japanese in Southeast Asia are often described as "puppet regimes," each headed by a nonentity whose main function was to implement orders emanating from Japan. A glance at the names of the "puppets" reveals how ill-informed this characterization is. The heads of the Japanese-sponsored governments of Burma (Ba Maw [1893–1977]), the Philippines (José Laurel [1891–1959]), and Indonesia (Sukarno [1901–1970]) were prominent men who, even after the defeat of Japan, continued to hold high positions in their countries. Subhas Chandra Bose (1897–1945?), the self-appointed president of Free India, was passionately devoted to Indian independence and certainly not a lackey of Japan. These men had decided that, whatever difficulties might result, cooperation with the Japanese offered the most likely possibility of ending colonial rule in their countries.

Freedom from colonial rule, more than enthusiasm for Greater East Asia, induced high-ranking persons from supposedly independent countries to attend conferences staged in Japan and to express in hyperbolic language their profound admiration for the emperor. They were not ignorant of the fact that the Japanese had refused to allow the inhabitants of Korea, Manchukuo (Manchuria), and Taiwan the freedom to choose their own governments. But they supported Japan, believing that Japan really meant its pledge to grant independence to the countries of the Greater East Asia Co-Prosperity Sphere. The celebrated opening of Okakura Kakuzō's *The Ideals of the East*, "Asia is one," was repeatedly quoted, as were such slogans as "Asia for the Asiatics."

The first important manifestation of the new pan-Asian spirit was the Daitōa Bungakusha Taikai (Greater East Asia Writers' Conference), which opened in Tokyo on November 1, 1942, the same month that the Greater East Asia Ministry was established. Yoshida Ken'ichi wrote his impressions:

The Congress of East Asian Writers was different in nature from the gatherings that are usually called "congresses." That such a meeting of writers was held in the midst of a great war is in itself unprecedented, but even more important, it is no exaggeration to say that it was a symbol of a movement in history and even of a transformation of the world: it is due to the war that men representing the literatures of different countries of Asia gathered in Japan for the first time and met the writers of our country. I often visited Teigeki,[18] the site of the congress, when there were displays of newly imported foreign art. Thinking back to those days, I realize that I never anticipated that such a day as this would occur, and though young, I cannot suppress a strange feeling that I have lived a very long time.

Among the gentlemen who came to Japan, I was struck by the attitude of the delegate from Mongolia, the first to speak. Mongol is an extremely monotonous language, and of course I could not understand a word. This was obviously true not only of myself, but he continued his speech without faltering. Later on, when I heard the Japanese translation, I realized that the Mongolian delegate's attitude was bolstered by his confidence and pride in ancient Mongol traditions. I was impressed. The same could be said of the speeches of the delegates from China and Manchuria. The delegates assembled this day represented countries with thousands of years of history and traditions.

I could not think of a single reason why we should not be their equal in the confidence and pride we feel in our own country's past. But haven't we for an excessively long time thought of the countries of Asia (apart from Japan) as foreigners or even enemies? The abstract theory that Asia is one (quite apart from the self-awakening of Okakura Kakuzō, who expounded this view) has been voiced even by Europeans in Europe. However, a realization that the incomparable fertility of East Asia, extending to both past and present, is one, just as Okakura said, has emerged from the present congress. I wonder if this is not its greatest achievement?[19]

It is difficult for me to imagine my friend Yoshida listening willingly to a speech delivered in a language he did not understand, especially one he characterized as monotonous. I am tempted to guess that his intent was parody; but the views expressed are in consonance with other articles he wrote at that time. Probably he wrote what he wanted to believe; many Japanese were happy to think of all Asia as one, even if they had an unfavorable opinion of every non-Japanese Asian they had ever met.

The Greater East Asia Writers' Conference was attended by fifty-seven delegates from Japan (including Korea and Taiwan) and twenty-six from China, Manchukuo, and Mongolia. As soon as the delegates from abroad arrived in Tokyo, they were taken to the Imperial Palace and the Meiji Shrine to pay their respects. On the following day, they worshipped at the Yasukuni Shrine. Japanese was the official language of the congress; speeches given in other languages were translated into Japanese, but those in Japanese were not translated into any other language. A delegate from Manchukuo declared, "Japanese has become the language of East Asia. East Asian literature, especially in Japanese, will shed its light throughout the world." A delegate from Taiwan chimed in, "Only by knowing the Japanese language can one come in contact with the great spirit of 'the eight corners of the world under one roof,' the guiding principle of East Asia."[20]

The second Greater East Asia Writers' Conference was held in Tokyo in August 1943 with the theme "The Annihilation of American and English Culture and the Establishment of the Culture of the Prosperity Sphere." The Japanese who attended the conference included fanatics like Fujita Tokutarō (1901–1945), a scholar of Japanese literature who launched an attack on Chinese who pronounced the characters of his name in any other way than *fuji-ta*.[21] The chairman of the meeting was the no less fiery Togawa Sadao (1894–1974). But other delegates were genuinely moved by the ideal of Asian writers working toward a common goal.

A different kind of Greater East Asia congress was held in Tokyo in November 1943; this time, the delegates were men of state rather than writers. Two countries, Burma and the Philippines, conquered by the Japanese, had recently been given independence, the Philippines less than a month earlier.[22] The Japanese-backed governments in China and Manchukuo had been recognized by the Japanese as independent for some years, though most of the world recognized only the Chinese government in Chungking. Thailand was the least enthusiastic country of Greater East Asia, perhaps because it had never been colonized; it sent not its prime minister but his deputy. Indonesia and Malaya were not invited because the Japanese military opposed granting independence—the theme of the congress—to countries whose natural resources were essential to Japan.[23] Subhas Chandra Bose, who on October 21, 1943, had founded the Indian National Army with the backing of the Japanese, was invited as an observer. There was some uncertainty about whether India belonged to Greater East Asia, but Bose described the congress as a "family party" at which all the guests were Asians.[24] Ba Maw, who attended as the head of state of Burma, wrote after the war, "Most of us were meeting for the first time, and yet we were behaving as if we had known each other all our lives, and had lost and now found one another again. Speaking for myself, I actually felt that it was no longer the Japan of my first visit; it was now Asia, and we were Asians rediscovering Asia."[25]

The congress opened on November 3, the birthday of Emperor Meiji, with a tea party hosted by Prime Minister Tōjō. The next morning, the delegates, who had spent the night in private homes rather than in hotels (because meals served in public places were meager), were met with Buicks and taken to the Imperial Palace. Emperor Hirohito welcomed the delegates, who responded with addresses of greeting. They did not present these addresses in *A, B, C* order of the names of the countries; if they had, Burma would have come first. If the usual Japanese order of *A, I, U, E, O* had been followed, China and Thailand would have preceded Japan. So the Japanese, in order to speak first, used the order found in the poem beginning *i-ro-ha-ni*, in which *ni* for "Nippon" comes before any other country. The same order was followed in all subsequent ceremonies.[26]

The theme of the congress, the independence of the countries of Greater East Asia, was featured in the "Pacific Charter," which was drawn up in response to the Atlantic Charter. Although the Atlantic Charter had declared that peoples have the right to determine their government, the end of colonial rule in Asia was not decreed or even termed desirable; this was the weakest aspect of the charter, and it was seized on by the Japanese. In April 1943, Shigemitsu Mamoru (1881–1957), the newly appointed foreign minister, had introduced the "liberation of Asia" as the war objective, thereby providing the Japanese with a noble cause that could unite all countries still under colonial rule.

All the delegates gladly accepted this principle, but on other issues there was disagreement and even resistance to Japanese policies. Although the delegate from Manchukuo, Chang Ching-hui, proudly recalled the speech delivered to the Diet by Prime Minister Tōjō in which he had said, "The prosperity and fulfillment of Manchukuo today reveals what all of Greater East Asia will be like tomorrow," the prospect of their countries becoming like Manchukuo, a country ruled largely by Japanese "advisers," was by no means welcome to all the delegates. Ba Maw of Burma and José Laurel of the Philippines, after paying the usual compliments to the Japanese, privately expressed opposition to "Manchukuoization."[27]

Laurel was in a particularly difficult position. Many Filipinos had been treated harshly by members of the Japanese army or the military police, and the Japanese had certainly not been welcomed as liberators.[28] On this occasion, he opened his remarks with the following: "As I entered your reception room, tears flowed from my eyes and I felt strengthened and inspired and said, 'One billion Orientals; one billion peoples of Greater East Asia! How could they have been dominated, a great portion of them, particularly by England and America?'"[29]

Laurel declared that the great empire of Japan, in order to enable the peoples and nations of Greater East Asia "to enjoy the natural right to live," was sacrificing life and property "and is staking its very existence in this sacred war." He would later state that by cooperating with the Japanese he had saved the Filipinos from great abuse. But in a meeting with Tōjō, he refused to declare war against the United States, saying that "it would not be 'decent' for the Filipinos to declare war against the United States that was their benefactor and ally."[30] Laurel could not ignore the dislike of his people for Japanese rule.

Ba Maw, as he wrote in a memoir published after the war, resented the barbarous acts committed by the Japanese military in the process of pacifying his country[31] and the numerous arrests afterward, but he had believed the Japanese promise of independence, and anything was better than a return of the British.[32] He stated, "For years in Burma I dreamt my Asiatic dreams. My Asiatic blood has always called to other Asiatics. In my dreams, both sleeping and waking, I have heard the voice of Asia calling to her children."[33]

U Nu, the first prime minister of Burma after the war and a major force for democracy at a time when it was menaced from both left and right, published in September 1944 an article in which he declared,

> Japan, as the champion and exponent of Mongolian racial resurgence, has succeeded in destroying the domination and influence of the Anglo-Saxon powers in the East. . . . It is the duty of all Asiatics . . . to participate in the destruction of the Anglo-

Saxon influence in the East and in the maintenance of a united front against attempts to re-encroach on Asiatic soil by anti-Asiatic races. . . . If Japanese hegemony in the Co-Prosperity Sphere means, and from what we have seen of her actions we fully believe it to mean, that the nations of East Asia shall get a fair deal in economic, political and social fields, then we shall and do welcome such leadership with hope and trust and faith, whatever the detractors may say. . . . And in the building of this Co-Prosperity Sphere, the thousand million people of East Asia can count themselves extremely fortunate in having such far-sighted, brilliant, and absolutely trustworthy leaders as General Tojo.[34]

Jorge B. Vargas, the wartime Filipino ambassador to Japan, stated in a radio address to his countrymen in January 1943:

The time has come for the Filipinos to discard Anglo-Saxon civilization and its enervating influence to effect a revolutionary change in their way of life, and to recapture their charm and original virtues as an oriental people. It is for you to begin the evolution of a new national culture than can make the Philippines a worthy and respectable member of the Co-Prosperity Sphere.[35]

The Joint Declaration of Greater East Asia was signed by all parties on November 6 in the presence of the ambassadors of Germany, Italy, Hungary, Bulgaria, Romania, Spain, and Denmark.[36] The congress had been carried out with admirable precision and effectiveness, and the signing of the declaration was given great prominence in the newspapers. But the congress, because it was so clearly focused on political matters, did not inspire literary commemoration. The activities of the Nihon Bungaku Hōkoku Kai (Japanese Literature Patriotic Association), often abbreviated as Bunpō, were more conspicuous.

The Bunpō, which had grown out of various organizations of writers,[37] had the strong backing of the wartime government. At the inauguration ceremony on May 26, 1942, the keynote address was delivered

by Okumura Kiwao (1900–1969), the assistant director of the Naikaku
Jōhōkyoku (Cabinet Information Bureau) and the author of *Sonnō jōi
no kessen* (*The Decisive Battle for Respect to the Emperor and Expulsion of
the Barbarians*). Okumura's use of the patriots' slogan of the 1860s ex-
emplified his fierce nationalism and xenophobia.

The long list of writers who belonged to the Bunpō gives the impression that everyone joined. Many did, whether out of sincere conviction
in its wartime aims or because being a member could redeem men with
records of leftist leanings from the sins of their past. But others stub-
bornly refused to join. Nagai Kafū received a letter from the Bunpō
strongly urging him to become a member, but he threw it away without
bothering to answer.[38] Uchida Hyakken (1889–1971), whose diary
Tōkyō shōjin (*Tokyo Reduced to Ashes*) is filled with vivid descriptions of
life during the bombings of Tokyo, was repeatedly approached but,
having made up his mind from the start not to join the Bunpō, managed
to maintain his independence.[39] Hyakken detested writers who con-
sorted with politicians.

Takami Jun resisted joining until July 1945, when he wrote in his
diary,

> The other day when Kon Hidemi urged me to join the Bunpō, I
> foolishly answered that I didn't mind. Kon himself, after being
> pressured again and again, had finally accepted, and now he
> asked me to join him. Kume [Masao] also urged me to join, and
> I carelessly said I would. Afterward, when I thought it over, I real-
> ized I didn't like the idea. I made up my mind that when a formal
> invitation arrived, I would refuse. The Bunpō, having heard from
> Kon that I had agreed to join, apparently put this on the agenda
> for the next meeting of the board of directors. Joining the Bunpō
> didn't bother me, but the loss of time for my studies would be
> painful. Perhaps this was a case of what Shimaki [Kensaku]
> calls "self-righteousness," but I was busy with "self-attainment." I
> should have refused external activity that would take me from
> my desk. I couldn't very well do that. I decided I would do only
> what fitted into the category of "unavoidable." It would be a relax-

ation, a ventilation of the spirit. But joining the Bunpō could not be merely a ventilation.[40]

Although he does not say so, Takami may have welcomed the salary he would receive from the Bunpō. He failed to mention that ten years earlier he had been arrested and tortured by the police as a suspected Communist. Clearing his name may have been another factor in his decision to join the Bunpō. Miyamoto Yuriko (1899–1951), an avowed Communist, when rebuked after the war for having joined the Bunpō by her husband, Miyamoto Kenji (1908–2007), who had been imprisoned as a Communist, said that she had found it unbearably lonely being on the outside.

Others would attempt after the war to excuse their participation in the activities of the Bunpō. The critic Hirano Ken (1907–1978) claimed that he had "accidentally" joined. But his section chief (a man about whom Hirano had nothing favorable to report in his reminiscences) declared that Hirano had begged him profusely, three times in his office and twice at his home, to find a place for him, even though there was no vacancy in that section of the Bunpō. When the section chief at last managed to obtain a post for him, Hirano traveled all the way to Kyūshū to convey his joy to his parents.[41] His joining the Bunpō was hardly "accidental."

It is extremely difficult to decide at this distance who was telling the truth in this and similar disputes. Suffice it to say that almost every recognized writer, willingly or not, became involved in the work of the Bunpō. It should be noted also that during the almost four years of its existence, the Bunpō accomplished remarkably little. Apart from sponsoring two congresses of writers, it published in May 1943 the *Aikoku hyakunin isshu* (*Patriotic Hundred Poems by a Hundred Poets*), arranged a celebration by haiku poets of the 250th anniversary of the death of Bashō, and raised funds to build a warship.[42]

F
A
L
S
E

V
I
C
T
O
R
I
E
S

A
N
D

R
E
A
L

D
E
F
E
A
T
S

THE BATTLES fought during the second half of 1943, mainly in the
Solomon Islands and New Guinea, did not arouse in the diarists the
excitement and grief of Guadalcanal and Attu. Takami Jun does not
even mention in his diary the fighting in the Solomon Islands. He
devoted barely a line to the loss of Makin and Tarawa in the Gilbert
Islands before passing on to an account of his discussion with an editor
about illustrations for his newspaper serial.

Itō Sei, however, never forgot the war. He wrote in his diary, "It is
certain that our men on Tarawa and Makin will all perish. They will
have made this sacrifice for the Imperial Land and for our race. The
land of Japan, where as autumn turns into winter the beauty of Fuji

becomes visible, is protected by the blood of these men."[1] He asked himself,

> Will the Anglo-Saxon race, which has established on the American continent the biggest materialistic culture, turn Asia into colonies under its rule, or will the Yamato race, devoted to the Asian ideal of the finest men dying for their country, lead the billion Asians of every belief and defend Asia to the end? The race is living through a fearful, decisive battle.
>
> The Americans excel at manufacturing, but when it comes to fighting, no people is the match of the Japanese. The manner in which the Japanese are now fighting is the best possible today, and it is succeeding.[2]

Itō took solace from official reports of enormous losses sustained by the American fleet, but when he learned that the Americans had landed on Rendova, one of the Solomon Islands, he exploded: "We must kill every last man in the American landing force, in this way avenging Guadalcanal and breaking the enemy's will to fight. . . . If, after what happened on Guadalcanal and Attu, we do not now teach a lesson to the enemy who has landed on a third island, our people may become discouraged."[3]

Itō may sound bloodthirsty, but not long afterward his hostility seemed justified by an article he read about Joseph Grew, a former American ambassador to Japan, who had allegedly said that the only way to deal with the Japanese was to kill them.[4] Itō declared, "There is definitely something in the blood of the Americans that delights in such irrational utterances. It is the blood that the people acquired and perfected when they slaughtered the natives in the process of opening up the New World."[5]

The Americans leveled the charge of cruelty against the Japanese, depicting them in cartoons as fanged monsters; Itō considered cruelty to be characteristic of the Americans. He quoted an American who looked forward to the day when Americans would wipe out not only every human being in Japan, but every tree and blade of grass.[6]

Later in the year, Itō was incensed by an editorial in the New York *Daily News* that declared that because the Japanese forces refused to surrender, the only way to defeat them was to drop poison gas on Tokyo and the suburbs. Itō cried out, "This is something the Yamato race must remember! What a thing to come out with publicly! This must be set down in history. They think the Anglo-Saxons are the only human beings. If they start using poison gas, their sons and brothers on islands of the Pacific will die of the poison gas we use against them."[7]

Kiyosawa Kiyoshi described in his diary a train trip he had taken to Hokkaidō. A volunteer corps was aboard, and at one point its leader shouted, "The Atlantic Charter was something put together by Churchill and Roosevelt. They've made up their minds to kill the entire Japanese population. Each and every man and woman will die. Are we going to let ourselves be killed by such people?" Kiyosawa added that it was commonly believed that if the Americans were victorious, they would prevent the birth of future Japanese by castrating all Japanese men or sending them into exile on distant islands.[8]

Developments in Europe contributed to Itō's distress:

July 27. I was astonished to learn from the morning paper that Mussolini has resigned. Italy is close to collapse. Mussolini was the man who built present-day Italy. Mussolini *was* Italy. It looks as if a part of the Axis is about to defect from the battle. This is a calamity. Under the headline the newspaper added an uncalled-for note, "No change in war policy," but I felt rage sweeping over me. If Mussolini is no longer in charge of state business, will this not endanger Hitler?[9]

Itō, who had believed that fascism would last forever, was "forlorn and saddened" when he read of recent developments in Italy.[10] He wrote in August 1943: "People like myself feel intuitively that it would be better to die than to live as members of a defeated country. This for a Japanese is instinctive; so if the Americans and British think of us in the same way they think of the Italians, they will find they have made a big mistake."[11]

Itō's hero was Adolf Hitler. On reading the text of a speech delivered by Hitler at the beer house in Munich where twenty years earlier he had founded the Nazi Party, Itō wrote,

> On reading it, I felt the conviction grow stronger that the man who made the speech was a genius. His ability to grasp people's hearts is magnificent. . . . I think it is splendid when an individual has convictions and both the ability to guide the people and the strength to make them believe. The present war, demolishing the conception of man as something weak (the teaching of the democratic, social thought in vogue since the nineteenth century) . . . has discovered supreme value in strength of will, dignity of character, and the beauty of the human being.[12]

Itō was appalled when an attempt was made on his hero's life.[13] Needless to say, he was unaware of the atrocities perpetrated at Hitler's command, but perhaps even if he had known, he might have excused the inhuman measures taken by Japan's ally as necessary in order to win the war.

Itō was not alone in these views. The outstanding tanka poet of the twentieth century, Saitō Mokichi (1882–1945), published an editorial in the principal tanka journal, *Araragi*, in which he wrote,

> The July 20th incident—the attempted assassination of the Reichsführer Adolf Hitler—has caused us all extreme concern. Why should the Germans, whom we have all trusted, have done such a thing? It is really most upsetting. . . . Even supposing Hitler lacks military genius, the assassins *should have realized what would happen to Germany if they succeeded in killing the Führer.*[14]

Ishikawa Jun (1899–1987) wrote in 1942 that, as far as Germany was concerned, Hitler was unquestionably a splendid leader, and even if by some mischance he should fail, it would be a beautiful failure.[15] Some Japanese writers at this time echoed the Germans in denouncing the Jews, blaming them for the evils of both capitalism and Communism.

A few Japanese doubted the Germans' commitment to the alliance. Kiyosawa noted on December 15, 1943: "The eleventh was the anniversary of the German-Japanese Offensive-Defensive Pact. Why is it celebrated only in Japan? In Berlin, Ambassador Ōshima [Hiroshi], as host, apparently invited high officials to attend the celebration, but [Joachim von] Ribbentrop did not show up."[16]

Itō was sure that even without the Germans, the Yamato race, regardless of setbacks, would in the end prove to be invincible. He wrote in July 1944:

This will be the year when the Yamato race comes face-to-face with a genuine crisis. I believe in the eternity of the Divine Land, and there has been no change in my absolute confidence in the invincibility of the Imperial soldiers, but we face increasing hardships; the bombing of our capital can be foreseen; and our allies in Europe are little by little being subjected to pressure on all sides, causing us further problems. How can we break through this impasse? Yamato race, bestir yourself! This is the moment to use our full strength, carrying our lives to their ultimate objective of ensuring the honor and destiny of the land of our ancestors.[17]

Itō's diary is by no means devoted exclusively to war cries and admonitions directed at the Yamato race.[18] He worried constantly about the possibility that he might be drafted despite his poor health. At first, he comforted himself with the thought that in a year and a half he would be forty, the maximum age for a man to be drafted; but before long, he heard rumors that the draft would soon be extended to include men up to forty-five. Alarmed by this possibility, he took a job teaching in a secondary school.[19]

Again and again, he also recorded increasing difficulty in supporting his family: "There is no money in the house. We have enough to pay the rice dealer and the postal insurance, which they'll be coming for today or tomorrow, but there's no money for anything else, and I'm worried. I've made up my mind I'll earn some money by writing by the end of the month a story about little girls or something for a children's magazine."[20]

The plight of writers was real. Magazines that normally would have asked Itō for manuscripts went out of business, either because of financial difficulties or because governmental edicts had required several magazines to merge or cease publication. Two leading magazines read by intellectuals, *Chūō kōron* and *Kaizō*, were banned in July 1944, presumably because they had remained relatively liberal in content. The reduction in the number of magazines resulted in the loss of income for writers, who had to find other work in order to feed their families. Itō worked for a time as an English teacher, but the government decided, in keeping with the war emergency, to end the teaching of the humanities, thereby depriving Itō of his job. He wondered how long he could continue to make a living as a writer. The novelist Kitahara Takeo (1907–1977) told Itō that literature was at a standstill; the only value the authorities recognized in writing was as propaganda.[21]

Itō anticipated that extremists in the publishing world (he did not consider himself to be one), as well as in the government, would make survival as an author difficult for anyone who, like himself, had studied Western literature. He decided that if he was ordered to keep silent about present conditions, he would do so; he would devote himself to writing about an uncontroversial subject like the Russo-Japanese War.[22] Still in the same mood a year later, he decided to change the content of his diary: "I will include clippings of newspaper reports on battles instead of writing much about them. I will try to avoid commenting on the war situation. I will, insofar as possible, not mention food shortages. I will write mainly about my work raising chickens and vegetables and my reflections on life."[23] Itō did not obey his own prescription. He decided toward the end of 1944 that it had become his mission to transmit to posterity what life was like for the Japanese during the war years. He vowed to keep writing the diary until the day he was sent to the battlefield. In fact, he continued the diary until the war ended in the unimagined Japanese defeat.[24]

Itō's conviction that the Yamato race would win the war was bolstered by official reports of stunning Japanese victories at sea. On

November 9, 1943, he learned from the seven o'clock radio news that three enemy battleships had been sunk and another heavily damaged off Bougainville, the biggest of the Solomon Islands. Two cruisers and three destroyers also had been sunk. He could not restrain the "leap in his heart."[25] In fact, no American battleships had participated in this engagement. The task force included two cruisers, neither of them hit, and a destroyer that was heavily damaged. The Japanese suffered greater losses, one light cruiser and a destroyer sunk. The rest of the Japanese triumph was imaginary. Itō noted several days later that Colonel Frank Knox, the American secretary of the navy, had maintained complete silence concerning the Japanese victory.

Late in November, after the American operation against the Japanese-held Gilbert Islands was launched, Itō wrote in his diary, "Enemy reports frequently mention the losses they have sustained. Probably the losses have actually been much greater. They would seem to be trying to divert attention from the disaster they suffered off Bougainville, which they still keep secret."[26]

On December 2, he heard that the enemy had lost two more aircraft carriers in the Gilberts, making a total of seven carriers lost there. Adding these to the five carriers and four battleships lost at Bougainville, the destruction of ships had been enormous, but still the Americans said nothing. On March 2, 1944, he heard rumors that the Japanese had recently sunk five or six more battleships and carriers, but in the absence of an official announcement, Itō decided that the rumors may have been false, though it was possible that the authorities were deliberately keeping the victory a secret. Four days later, he heard a report that ten aircraft carriers had been sunk off the Bonin Islands, only to learn on March 10 from an editor that this naval victory had been a hoax. He guessed that the false rumor was a ruse by the enemy.[27]

Itō did not as the result of the deception become more cautious about accepting reports of sunken American ships. He joyfully described in his diary a naval battle off Taiwan and Okinawa on October 16, 1944. Imperial Headquarters officially proclaimed that ten enemy aircraft carriers, two battleships, three cruisers, and one destroyer had been sunk and nineteen other ships damaged. Itō termed this the greatest victory in all naval history. The Japanese had lost only one carrier. The American carriers, the main strength of the fleet, were now buried at the bottom of the sea. Sovereign power over the western Pacific was once again in the hands of the Yamato race. The fears that had lurked in the minds of the people were gone, and the dark atmosphere hanging over Japan had dissipated. There was general confidence that Japan had the strength to win any battle in which it participated. This change of feeling could be seen overflowing onto the streets, into the offices where people congregated, and even to people waiting in line for their rations. Prime Minister Koiso Kuniaki's (1880–1950) published interview on the victory was excellent.

Itō declared that as the result of this triumph, the United States could never again defeat Japan in the Pacific:

> The enemy has flinched. Even if the enemy spends the next year or two building carriers and comes to attack, we shall be waiting for them, having replenished our strength in the meantime. The Japanese, who know no defeat except fighting to the death, will become all the more unshakable in their confidence. In the course of a battle that lasted three or four days, we have made the Americans taste a defeat like that of the Germans, crushed at Stalingrad after an invasion of six months. The decisive battle was fought in an unbelievably short time. I would like to tell our men who committed *gyokusai* not only on Saipan, Tinian, and Guam but on Attu, the Gilbert Islands, Kwajalein, Ruot, and other places what has happened.[28]

What Itō called the greatest victory in naval history is not described as such in any subsequent work. In fact, it never happened. Itō and the rest of the Japanese were exhilarated by news of the destruction of the American fleet, but in the battle off Taiwan and Okinawa fought between October 12 and 16, 1944, only two American cruisers were damaged. No American ships were sunk, and the loss of 312 Japanese fighter-bombers in attacks on the American fleet permanently deprived the Japanese of control of the air. Japanese reconnaissance pilots, flying after the supposedly stunning defeat of the Americans, discovered to their surprise that the fleet was virtually intact, but it was too late to retract the news of victory. On October 21, the emperor issued a message of congratulations to the commanding officers. He, too, had been led to believe the bloated reports of enemy losses.

Reasons have been given to try to explain why the Japanese were so mistaken in their estimates of the damage they had dealt the American ships, but perhaps the simplest explanation is that a victory was needed at this stage of the war. At the beginning of the war, when the Americans were staggered by successive Japanese victories, there seemed to be one bright spot: the sinking of the battleship *Haruna* by an intrepid aviator, Colin Kelly, who flew his plane into the smokestack of the Japanese ship. President Roosevelt recommended that when the infant son of the late aviator reached college age, he be admitted to West Point. It was reported that Kelly had received the Congressional Medal of Honor, the highest American military decoration.[29] When I arrived in Pearl Harbor early in 1943, I was told as a secret that the *Haruna* was still afloat and had not even been damaged. I cannot recall any public avowal of the mistaken report, which seems to have been intended as an antidote to prevailing gloom. The air raid on Tokyo by bombers under the command of James Doolittle probably had the same purpose; certainly the damage inflicted on Japan did not compensate for the lost lives and planes.

Itō, however, was perturbed to read the statement by Secretary of the Navy James V. Forrestal that, because of the greatly increased strength of the U.S. Navy, two of the four fleets in the Pacific would be sufficient to deal with the entire Japanese fleet. If this was true, Itō wrote in his diary, perhaps the Japanese navy was not as strong as people were often told. He confessed to being a little worried, but took comfort from the fact that the biggest American carrier fleet had been wiped out. Itō concluded, "The motives behind the pronouncements of enemy politicians can generally be seen through quite easily. I often feel they are like children showing off their prowess."[30]

A development that would have serious implications for the safety of American ships gave Itō special satisfaction. He wrote on October 29:

According to yesterday morning's newspaper, the kamikaze Special Attack Force, whose mission is to crash into enemy warships, has made its appearance.... I've heard quite often from about a month back about planes being built that were not intended to return.

Now they have manifested themselves, a symbol of the supreme spiritual strength of the Japanese race. If Japan cannot win the war, even with this strength, it will be a negation of the existence of the spiritual powers of human beings, and can only mean that humankind has plunged into the dark domination of the power of material production. No—the Japanese, with this spiritual power, will without question fight through to victory.... This is the supreme achievement of the Japanese.[31]

Other writers would also glorify the Special Attack Force (*tokkōtai*).[32] The novelist Yokomitsu Riichi (1898–1947) wrote an essay typical of the tributes to the Special Attack Force pilots. It opens

Spirit that keeps separating from everything else—what manner of thing might this be? Probably no matter how anyone might attempt to discover a way to define it, the spirit of the Special Attack Force that day after day sets off from its base cannot be defined. It is not a matter simply of one man causing an enemy warship to sink. It is hitting a target with one's death. But that definition is also mistaken. It is serving one's country with one's body. No, that's not it either. In that case, what is it?

I believe that the spirit of the Special Attack Force is the expression of the purest world spirit, transmitted from antiquity, thousands of years, perhaps tens of thousands of years back. If it were simply a matter of the fighting spirit needed to destroy the enemy or anything similar, it would not be necessary to separate the spirit from everything else. If it were a matter of a spirit of resignation, yielding to whatever fate might bring, there would be no need for training. I believe it is not so much a spirit of creating history but of sustaining the spirit of creation, the loftiest spirit of morality, but even saying this does not approach the reality.[33]

The Special Attack Force and its successes in sinking or damaging American ships brought hope to Itō and other diarists, but Itō wrote on January 18, 1945:

> The military situation in the Philippines, despite all the bombast in the newspapers, is definitely not good. The enemy is advancing southward from Lingayen through the Luzon plain to Manila. . . . The enemy has begun to use the airfield at Lingayen for light planes. This means that control of the air has gradually fallen into the hands of the enemy.
>
> How can we, without planes or ships, get the upper hand in our fight for the Philippines? At present the politicians, the officials, the industrialists, with only a faint spirit of working for their country, speak in passionate tones that we have no chance of winning the war.[34]

The last phrases strike a new note: defeatism had come to worry him. When Itō went to the Bunpō on February 8, 1945, he heard that the Japanese army on Leyte had been wiped out:

> I had been so absorbed by the fighting on Luzon that I hadn't been paying attention to Leyte. Up to this month, the battle for Leyte was reported in detail, but then reports stopped appearing in the newspapers. I hear there was a *gyokusai* on Leyte about ten days ago. According to the people at the Bunpō today, the food and ammunition of our army on Leyte was stolen by the enemy, who had contrived to get to the rear of our army and annihilate it. Enemy broadcasts say that the Japanese army on the island, some 300,000 men, reduced to starvation, have become prisoners. I can't believe that, even if they were starving, hundreds of thousands of Japanese would willingly become prisoners. But the silence in our communiqués is ominous. . . .

The authorities often said that if we were defeated on Leyte, it would mean we had lost the war. The Special Attack Force has crashed into one enemy ship after another, sinking dozens of them, our shock troops have captured enemy airfields, and parachutists have carried out counter-attacks, but despite these glorious achievements, the whole island of Leyte was soon surrounded by the enemy, and the enemy moved farther north to Luzon and Mindoro. This was the point when news from Leyte came to a halt.[35]

Takami Jun was away from Japan during much of the war. At the outbreak, he was an army correspondent in French Indochina, and he spent all of 1942 in Burma. He returned to Japan in January 1943, but in 1944 he was sent to China, where he passed the second half of the year. His diary, though filled with accounts of people he met and with sketches of tourist attractions, does not say much about what he actually did as an army correspondent.

The most memorable event of Takami's stay in China in 1944 was the third Greater East Asia Writers' Conference, held in Nanking in November. The Japanese delegation was originally scheduled to be headed by the popular writer Mushakōji Saneatsu (1885–1976), but at the last moment he was taken ill and replaced by Nagayo Yoshirō (1888–1961),[36] who delivered an address entitled "How to Use Novels, Poetry, Plays etc. to Raise Morale and Enhance Fighting Spirit, and by Cooperating in the Greater East Asia War and Driving Out Britain and America, Bring About the Liberation of the Greater East Asian Peoples." Takami's speech had a more modest title: "How Shall We Raise the Cultural Level and the Racial Awareness of the Peoples of Greater East Asia?"[37]

Takami described the gathering in these terms:

The scene of the Congress was quite amusing.
    The Chinese were hardly listening. Once in a while, they would look up, but for the most part they read magazines or newspapers on their desks.

Their attitude was truly uninhibited. There was no sign of constraint or reserve. —I in fact envied them.

The Manchurian delegates all delivered speeches on such hackneyed themes as "Now we are faced with a severe decisive battle etc." There were many practical proposals from the Chinese intended to do something about the financial problems of men of culture.

The Japanese all brought manuscripts of the speeches they were to give. Their delivery was clumsy. The Chinese gave their talks with only memos to guide them. They spoke skillfully with abundant gestures. (This irritated me into not taking any notes with me for my talk.)[38]

Takami's diary of his visit to China is quite unlike the diaries kept at the time by writers in Japan. He hardly mentioned the war, and there was no shortage of food or fear of bombing. No aversion is expressed for the Japanese military he encountered, though he surely could not have forgotten how he had been arrested by the military in 1933 on suspicion of being a Communist. Takami had written a confession after being tortured by command of an officer know for his brutality.[39]

This description fits Amakasu Masahiko (1891–1945), an army officer responsible for the death of the anarchist Ōsugi Sakae (1885–1923). Amakasu was tried for the crime and found guilty, but after a brief imprisonment, he was sent to France for study. He was now making propaganda films in Manchukuo. Takami met Amakasu several times during his visit, but his diary contains not one word about his impressions.

The diary covering Takami's stay in China is of relatively minor interest, but once he was back in Japan the diary becomes invaluable as a day-to-day description of 1945, the end of the war and the beginning of the Occupation. China and Manchukuo (at least the places he visited) had been peaceful, and though prices were high, one could buy almost anything. Japan was gloomy, and the shops were empty. The first full-scale bombing of Tokyo took place on November 24, 1944, shortly before Takami returned from China. From then on, there was danger every day and night of air raids. People were afraid to go to the theaters because any large building was a likely target.[40]

Takami lived in Kamakura, about an hour's journey from Tokyo. It had not been bombed, but rumors circulated that the nearby coast was the most likely place for an American landing. The tension may have contributed to Takami's conviction that keeping this diary, a record not only of his personal life but of the agony of Japan, was his most important work. To make a living, he wrote for any publisher who asked for a manuscript, but the number kept dwindling. Despite the danger, Takami continued to visit Tokyo frequently, sometimes to put in an appearance at the Bunpō but more often to drink at whatever bars were still open. Maps in his diary show the locations of bars destroyed in the bombing, mementos of happier days.

Takami noticed on his train trips between Kamakura and Tokyo how seldom he saw students like those who used to make up the majority of the passengers. Even middle-school pupils had been conscripted for work in munitions factories.[41] When his train passed through Ōfuna, Takami saw women and children scrabbling among piles of ashes for coal that might still be burned. He commented, "In China, I saw such scenes everywhere." Although the Japanese looked down on the Chinese as backward, poverty and wartime shortages had driven even Japanese to desperate expedients.[42]

Takami nostalgically mourned neighborhoods that had been almost completely destroyed. He also related that the inhabitants of Tokyo had taken to eating *rakkyō* (pickled onions) with their breakfasts as one sure way to save themselves from bombs. (There was a condition: eating *rakkyō* was effective only if one informed acquaintances of its magical powers.)[43]

On February 27, 1945, Takami visited Tokyo and was stunned by the extent of the destruction. The whole area around Kanda Bridge had been burned, and in places smoke was still rising. The left side of Ogawa Street, which, when he last visited, had escaped burning, was now blackened ruins, and the right side, as far as the eye could see, was a wasteland. He had not even heard rumors about the devastation. He wondered if people he met, even if they knew about the damage, hesitated to speak. The diary entry continues:

> When I got back home, the newspapers had arrived. I felt inde-scribable rage at the newspapers for maintaining their silence about the tragedy of Tokyo. What are newspapers for? And this silence is not confined to the fires. I can understand that, because of counter-espionage and the like, they're not able to publish certain things, but it would be better not to deceive the people. Is it right for them not to trust the people—the people who, without shedding a tear at the burned-out sites, go about their work, bravely and admirably?[44]

Five months later, Takami wrote in the same vein:

> Yesterday I promised to meet Nakamura Murao and Shioya Ryōhei and go with them that afternoon to the Bunpō office. . . . I realized that no matter how long I waited at Tamachi, a streetcar bound for Meguro would never come. Then a little streetcar bound for Tengenji came creaking up. It was an indescribable wreck of a streetcar. Some foreigners were aboard. I wondered what the for-eigners thought of this broken-down streetcar and of the many dirty-looking Japanese on that streetcar. I considered all possi-bilities. In the end, I felt absolutely sure that they would think that the Japanese were holding up admirably. The little buildings of burned galvanized sheeting visible from the streetcar win-dows were also holding up admirably. I felt more cheerful. And deep in my heart I felt I didn't want these brave Japanese to be plunged into further suffering and unhappiness. I wonder if our war leaders have such affection. I wonder if they actually know the present state of things.[45]

ON DECEMBER 31, 1944, Nagai Kafū wrote in his diary, "Clear, followed by cloudy. Air-raid alarm at ten tonight. All clear immediately afterward. Frequent sounds of gunfire. 1944 is about to end and a dismal New Year to begin. Never before in the long history of our country has there been such a predicament. It's entirely the doing of the military. Their crimes must be recorded for all time to come."[1]

The year 1945 was bad not only for Kafū, but for all the inhabitants of Tokyo. The capture of the airfield on Iwo Jima brought the Americans within striking distance of Tokyo, and they soon stepped up the fire-bombing. One neighborhood after another was destroyed. The worst attack took place on the night of March 10. Kafū, who had seldom deigned to notice fires elsewhere in the city, this time was profoundly shocked by an irreparable loss. The Henkikan,[2] the house he had built and lived in for twenty-five years, a house filled with books he had bought in the United States and Europe, burned to the ground. His account of the disaster, describing the night of March 10, opens

> At four in the morning, my Henkikan burned. The fire started half-way up Nagatare Slope, then, fanned by a northwesterly wind, suddenly vaulted over to the main street in Ichibei. The window by my pillow grew bright in the light of the fires. Startled by the unusual shouting of my neighbors, I went out into the garden, taking with me in a satchel my diary and manuscripts. I watched the flames as they rose above Tanimachi. The sky far to the north reflected the fires. Sparks dancing in the strong wind cascaded into the garden. I looked in all directions, but thought I probably had no chance to escape. I ran out to the street through smoke that was already billowing.[3]

Kafū made his way to a police box. He asked if he could get through to Mita, where he had a friend. On being told that the fires made this unlikely, he set off in a different direction, but once again flames blocked him. Just then he saw a girl of seven or eight leading an old man by the hand. They were obviously lost. After guiding them to a safer place, he turned back for a last glimpse of the Henkikan, making his way with difficulty and ignoring cries of warning. When he reached the neighborhood, flames were rising so high over the house that he could not see it. His ten thousand books had gone up in smoke.

When it grew light, Kafū managed to reach the house of his cousin Kineya Gosō, where, worn out and aching from his wanderings, he fell asleep. He awoke to the realization that his house and books were gone and he had nothing now except the clothes on his back. He recalled that though he had lived in happy seclusion in the Henkikan for twenty-five years, wartime difficulties in finding people to clean the house and tend the garden had made him consider selling the house and the books and moving to an apartment. Perhaps losing everything in this way would actually provide the basis for a quiet old age, but he could not forget the books of poetry and novels he had bought during the past forty years. The thought that he could never again take them in his hands filled him with heartfelt regret.[4]

The next day, Gosō sent his sons to the Henkikan to "scrape through the ashes" and see if they could find anything. They returned with three items: a seal that Tanizaki Jun'ichirō had given to Kafū, a teacup of Raku ware that had belonged to his father, and the pipe that his maternal grandfather had smoked every day. There could be no more precious mementos. All three objects had miraculously escaped the fire unscathed.

Kafū did not express bitterness toward the Americans for destroying his house; what bitterness he felt was reserved for the militarists who had started the war.[5]

Other Japanese diarists felt far greater anger toward the enemy. Yamada Fūtarō described in his diary the desolation of Tokyo after the bombing—streets where he could tell from the thickness of the coating of gray dust sticking to the broken shop windows, from lopsided signs, and from fallen, peeled walls that the desolation was not the work of a single night's attack but the result of three dismal years of warfare: "Birds are not singing. No sign of spring grass. Clouds of sand hover above air-raid shelters dug up along the sidewalks. The cold sunlight of early spring is filled with nothing but nihilistic whiteness."[6] He continued,

> Last night at Meguro, I watched the B-29s as they slowly circled above the flames in the downtown area, scattering incendiary bombs like rain. Probably they do not recognize that the creatures living in the world below them are also members of the human race. No doubt they think of us as swarms of little yellow monkeys. Of course this is war. I will not voice the usual stupid indignation over the enemy's indiscriminate bombing or say that the gods won't tolerate such behavior, or anything of the sort. They are our enemies, and it is completely normal for them to wish to slaughter tens of thousands of Japanese.

That being the case, it is of course more than proper for us, too, to wish to slaughter hundreds of thousands of Americans. No, we must kill them; the more, the better.

We will become cool-headed. We will take an eye for an eye and a tooth for a tooth, like cold-blooded animals. Freezing our blood and our tears, we will study how to kill even one more of them. It won't be enough to drag down into hell an American for each Japanese who dies. We will kill three of them for each one of us. We will kill seven for two, thirteen for three. We can survive this war if every Japanese becomes a demon of vengeance.[7]

Yamada was twenty-three when he set down these sentiments. He and I were born in the same year. In some ways, we were alike. We had been moved by many of the same books. Yamada's diary records what he was reading even during periods of intense bombing. Usually he gave only the titles, without any personal comments, but on May 7 he wrote of Alexandre Dumas's *La Dame aux camélias*: "I wonder how many times I have read this book. This time, too, it seemed to me a masterpiece. It is not true that only old men of ripe experience can produce a masterpiece. It was precisely because the younger Dumas was twenty-four years old that his work is filled with dreams, beauty, joys and sorrow, and a passion of which no old man is capable."[8] I can imagine writing something similar in 1945 if I, like Yamada, had kept a diary.

Yamada read stories by Tolstoy, Chekhov, and Gorky, but his main interest (like mine) was French literature, especially the works of Balzac. At one point, I made the resolve, not fulfilled, of reading the entire *Comédie humaine*. Yamada probably read more of Balzac than I did. One work that Yamada read at this time particularly surprised me— *Pelléas et Melisande*, a play of delicate beauty set in a long-ago, far-away kingdom. My first reaction on reading this entry in his diary was that it was a strange work to read at a time of horrendous conflict. But then I recalled that when I landed on Okinawa in 1945, I had a copy of Racine's *Phèdre* in my knapsack.

Perhaps the greatest difference separating us was that I did not share his hatred for the enemy. Of course, I wanted the United States to win the war, but I felt warmly toward the Japanese prisoners I interrogated and some became friends. Instead of wishing that even one more Japanese would be killed in the fighting, I wished that even one more would be saved as a prisoner. Probably my lack of hatred was due, in part at least, to the fact that the Japanese had not destroyed the city where I lived, nor did I fear that they might occupy my country. I do not think, however, that I ever wished hundreds of thousands of Japanese to be slaughtered; the dropping of the atomic bombs profoundly shocked me.

Yamada, for all his expressed hatred, was not unaware that the Americans had good qualities. He attended a lecture on February 1, 1945, given by Dr. Suzuki Bunshirō, the managing editor of the *Asahi shimbun*,[9] on "National Characteristics of the Enemy" and transcribed in his diary the following points of Suzuki's lecture:

> The Americans are extraordinarily hard-working. Who in Japan works most efficiently today? Jailbirds and American prisoners. I don't know about jailbirds, but the Americans don't necessarily work hard because they have bayonets at their backs. They are a people who really enjoy working. Before the outbreak of the present war, I crossed the ocean to America and later went on to Europe. When I returned to America, my impression was that the European countries were at three in the afternoon, but America was at ten in the morning.

Suzuki praised Americans' organizational skill and recalled that it took only forty-five minutes to produce a new car at the Ford Motor Company. He was especially impressed by the cleanliness of the automobile factory and of the United States as a whole, contrasting it with his own country:

> In Japan, it is true, people diligently polish and cleanse their houses in the manner of a room for the tea ceremony. However, once they step outside, they behave in a most lamentable manner. They spit on the streets; they scatter paper handkerchiefs. In

extreme cases, as I saw the other day in an underground passage of Tokyo Station to my amazement and fury, a gentleman may brazenly urinate against a wall. Parks and hospitals, which should be the most beautiful and cleanest places, are the most unsanitary. The Ministry of Education is splendid on the outside, but inside it is like a village office in its filth and muddle. It is shocking to think that this is the center of education in Great Japan.[10]

If an American lecturer at this time had described the good qualities of the Japanese, he, exactly like Suzuki characterizing the Americans, probably would have stressed their devotion to their work and their cleanliness. Suzuki, after praising American courage, added, "When their courage takes a wrong direction, it is apt to turn into violence and brutality"—a charge that the Americans equally applied to the Japanese. Captured Japanese documents that I read often contained evaluations of the merits and demerits of American soldiers. They were very similar to the evaluations of Japanese soldiers made by the Americans.

Yamada, though a noncombatant, presented the choice that faced the Japanese soldiers:

> To fight and in so doing destroy the country? Or to yield and be smeared with eternal shame? This is a truly terrifying choice between life and death. It is by no means the kind of simple proposition one finds in novels. It is a battle between the instinct to preserve one's life and an intellectual desire for glory. It is a duel between the animal and the divine within the human body. Which will the Japanese choose?

He answered this question with a command: "Never surrender, no matter what happens! Be a people with a sense of shame who do not fear death!"[11]

Yamada's high-minded advice to the Japanese was not confined to those living in Japan. When he learned of the Germans' surrender to the Allies, he expressed the hope that Japanese residents in different

parts of Europe would take their own lives, rather than become prisoners of the British and Americans. He contrasted the Japanese readiness
to die with the German willingness to surrender, and suggested that
these differences would lead to two different courses of action for the
Americans:

> Our enemies, the Americans, fearing the huge sacrifice of lives if
> they make a direct attack on Japan, may adopt the strategy of
> landing in China, in this way isolating Japan and causing it to
> self-destruct. Or they may attack the Japanese homeland with
> one powerful blow and, by destroying the center, cause the out-
> lying regions to fall. The greater likelihood of one rather than the
> other has been much discussed, but whichever they choose, the
> Americans will find that Japan, unlike Germany, is unchanging
> and unyielding. If the enemy attempts to apply to Japan the tac-
> tics they used with the Germans, we will be obliged to reward
> their misapprehension with a mortal wound.[12]

Yamada foresaw new possibilities of conflict:

> The Soviet Union must ultimately fight with Japan; this is pre-
> destined. Now, while Japan is desperately battling in the Pacific,
> is the most advantageous time for them to launch an attack on
> Manchuria behind Japan's back. It is entirely to be expected that
> the Soviet Union should think in these terms. At present, the
> hands of the Soviet Union are free, while America is still fight-
> ing Japan. Not one Japanese soldier has as yet surrendered, and
> whenever an island is attacked by America, the entire garrison
> fights to the death and commits *gyokusai*. As long as America is
> occupied with such a troublesome enemy, it will be an unbear-
> able strain to take on the Soviet Union, free to do whatever it
> pleases in Europe, which has suffered such extreme sacrifices.
> It can easily be imagined how the worries not only of Japan but
> of America will be utilized to the maximum by that frightening
> realist Stalin. . . . The Soviet Union desires a situation in which

Japan and America go on fighting desperately until both are exhausted. If they think that Japan is in danger, they may actually resuscitate Japan so it will continue to fight America. One can't say this won't happen. In that case, Japan and the Soviet Union may team together in a strange alliance to fight America, Britain, and Germany.[13]

Yamada was impressed by Vsevolud Ivanov's story "Hungry Ghosts," about some Russians who carry off a Kirghiz woman in order to obtain her milk for a Russian baby. A Russian decides to kill the woman's infant so that the Russian baby will have all her milk. When she attempts to save her child's life, he asks, "You want a Russian boy to die for that infidel?" Yamada was aware that Ivanov's purpose was to depict the inhuman brutality of the Russian, and it led him to ask, "Is not this war of Japan's, consciously or unconsciously, the vengeance of the yellow men exacted against such white men?"[14]

Despairing of finding anywhere to live in Tokyo, Yamada decided to return to his home in the San'in region. There were extremely few trains, and after he had waited for four hours, the train that arrived was already full. People were sitting and squatting everywhere, three people to a seat and some perched on the armrests. The train arrived in Kyoto eleven hours later, at ten o'clock in the morning. Yamada had to wait until three in the afternoon for the only train for the San'in. While waiting he read, on the platform of the San'in line, Balzac's *Le Lys dans la vallée*.

Yamada, by chance, met a friend named Takuma, with whom he shared a canteen of saké. They expressed dismay over the course of the fighting on Okinawa. The main islands would inevitably be the next battlefield. But they were sure that if every last soldier fought to the death, Japan could still win.[15]

Takuma said that a new weapon, a deadly light ray, had been perfected. Yamada had heard rumors of the Sakura No. 5, a fighter designed to shoot down B-29s, and of a squadron of planes that was ready to bomb the American mainland; but he thought that such rumors were dubious. If there really was a plane that could shoot down B-29s, it would have to make its appearance fairly soon, or there would not be anything left of Japan to save. At any rate, Japan should not follow the example of Germany, which had gone down to defeat while dreaming of new weapons.[16]

The tone of Yamada's diary is gloomy. As a person trained in the sciences, he discounted rumors based only on desperation, but he was unable to think objectively about Japan's chances in the war. On May 21, a B-29 scattered propaganda leaflets in the Kanda area of Tokyo. Yamada heard that the leaflets accused the military clique of having started the invasion of Manchuria without obtaining the emperor's consent, and advised the Japanese that their only solution was to surrender.[17] Yamada did not suggest a reply to this charge. Instead, he gave reasons why the Japanese should not consider becoming prisoners, citing reports that German war criminals were being sent as slaves to the Soviet Union, the United States, Great Britain, and France, to rebuild those countries. He predicted nevertheless that Germany would enjoy vengeance in a few dozen years.[18] He did not, however, predict that if Japan was defeated, it, too, would some day take vengeance. He could not mention the possibility of defeat.

Uchida Hyakken's diary, by contrast, is prevailingly cheerful. His house was spared the firebombing of March 10, but though he was well aware that his neighborhood might be the next to be devastated, he refused to leave the city. His most persistent concern was obtaining a sufficient supply of cigarettes and saké. He wrote on April 4, 1945:

Iwo Jima has been taken, and I hear that the enemy army has landed on Okinawa. This means that raids by enemy planes will become much more frequent. But it occurred to me that when the all clear has sounded after a raid that was frightening enough to shorten one's life, and one thinks with relief that one has survived unscathed another raid, how nice it would be to have some saké or beer. That's all I think about each time.[19]

Hyakken's good luck with the bombing did not last forever. A large-scale raid took place on the night of May 25. Hyakken wrote,

The air-raid siren sounded at 10:23. We again moved outside the house the bundles of our belongings we had left by the front door early yesterday morning. Tonight seemed likely to be dangerous. All at once, the sky to the southwest turned a pale red. Even more disturbing was the gradual increase in the number of enemy planes flying overhead. One of them fell, spewing forth flames. Incendiary bombs began to fall nearby. Massive B-29s came flying from the direction of Yotsuya and Ushigome on the other side of the embankment, at a lower altitude than ever before. The fuselage of the planes and the undersides of their wings were dyed red, rather like the underbelly of a newt, reflecting the color of the city in flames. Though I kept thinking that I shouldn't, I went on staring at the planes as they passed directly overhead. The thudding echoes of bombs being dropped could be heard in quick succession.[20]

The raid lasted until one o'clock in the morning. When they heard the all clear, Hyakken and his wife were happy still to be alive. They did not go back to look at their house. They knew that it undoubtedly had been totally destroyed. There was no point in bewailing their losses, but Hyakken could not help but regret losing a scroll in the hand of the great novelist Natsume Sōseki. He managed to save some essentials, including a partly consumed bottle of saké, carefully stored in his pack.

Hyakken and his wife had nowhere to go, but they found a hut where they could at least pass the night, though it had no water, electricity, toilet, or kitchen. Despite the uncertainty of survival, he spent the following day catching up on the diary he had lately neglected. This done, he and his wife considered their options. They could leave the city for a less dangerous place, but that would make it difficult for him to reach the office where he worked, and he obviously could not make a living in the country. They might try, as others had, to make their home in an air-raid shelter, but once the summer rains started it would be miserable. They decided to remain in the hut "until the war clouds had abated." When the owner of the hut offered to clear a room in his house for the couple, they politely refused.[21] Hyakken valued his freedom too much to accept kindness in adversity. The same desire to avoid entanglements had made him refuse to join the Bunpō.[22]

On May 30, the streetcars were running again. Hyakken went to Yotsuya Station to set his watch by the station clock, but the clock had stopped because of a power failure. As he slowly walked back to the hut where he now lived, he recalled that he had often read in the newspapers of people who had felt a kind of relief after being burned out of their houses. Hyakken's situation was rather different, but he also felt relief:

> I recalled the area around the big desk in my study upstairs, the insides of the bookcase drawers, the closets, the top of the little table in the hall off the living room. They were all cluttered with the tedious business matters I had always thought I would some day put in order and dispose of but never had. It gave me a really marvelous feeling to think that the flames had liberated me from everything in one stroke.[23]

Watanabe Kazuo, a distinguished professor at Tokyo University, began to keep a diary on March 11, the day after the catastrophic air attack. He wrote most of the entries in French, but phrases in Italian, Latin, and other languages also appear, always tragic in content. The cover of the diary bears two quotations: "Lasciate ogni speranza" and "Mane, Thecel, Pharès!!" The first, "Abandon all hope," is from *The Divine Comedy*, the inscription above the gates of hell; the second, from the Bible (Daniel 5:25–28), are the words on the wall that warned of the terrible fate awaiting a country given to impious behavior. It is hard to imagine a more despondent outlook.

The diary proper opens with an account of why Watanabe had kept a diary but abandoned it because he thought that nothing he could write would be of interest to those who survived him:

> Today I began to write again. This change has come about because I have found some hope and convincing enough reason for me to take up my pen. The smallest facts, whether insignificant

or terrible, the notes and thoughts that I shall record here, will surely be of use for *my second life*, my resurrection when I shall have my *vengeance*; the word came spontaneously, so strong and well-nourished is my resolve.

The bombardment on the night of the ninth of March destroyed my beloved old Hongō neighborhood. All my memories and all my dreams are forever destroyed. I must endure trial after trial. I must think of the despair of the Man at Calvary. Compared with Him, I am a nameless little beast, coarse and cowardly. These trials are nothing alongside His grief. Endure!

Mater dolorosa![24]

Some entries, like the following, are unique among writers' diaries of the time:

If I am obliged to take up a bamboo spear, I will go where I'm told to go. But I will definitely not kill an American. I will voluntarily become a prisoner.

I curse those who have swelled our people's pride. This is the source of all our unhappiness.[25]

Watanabe's translation of Rabelais had just been printed and bound when the printing house was hit during a bombing and every copy burned. His only comment was, "Rabelais had no connection with Japan, after all." This expression of resignation is followed by "Japan does not crave anything. It is unbelievably indifferent to gain. It has even abandoned hope of giving birth to people who are splendid citizens of the world. Ruination. This seems to be its sole hope and prayer." Later the same day, he wrote, "The weakness of the intellectuals, or perhaps their cowardliness, was fatal. This is what makes one think that there are no real intellectuals in Japan. The intellectuals should be strong and courageous in order to protect the freedom to think and the integrity of thought."[26]

On March 16, Watanabe received a letter from Miyahara Kōichirō,[27] who wrote that the day of men of his age has ended, and that the time has come to prepare a movement of cultural reconstruction. He hoped that men of Watanabe's generation would lead the still younger men. But few old persons thought in such terms. Watanabe wrote, "My aged father is obstinate. He has no conception of the menacing, critical situation of our country. He vegetates, it seems to me, clinging to a belief in the certainty of victory, as if he were still living in the long-ago past."[28]

The old slogans, promising certain victory, were still much on display, but Watanabe, compiling (in the manner of Flaubert) a new "dictionary of received ideas," gave the slogans sardonic interpretations, including "The eight corners of the world under one roof. Meaning: If you don't listen to what I say, I'll kill you, I'll burn you alive." He defined "a special attack force of the hundred millions" as "let the whole world perish without a single cry of protest," and gave the sacred *gyokusai* a new definition as "death out of despair."[29]

Watanabe heard that there was at the Ministry of Foreign Affairs a list of Japanese war criminals, compiled in Chungking. He commented, "They don't want to die for us, for the people. They want to die with us, dragging us by force and trickery into the abyss."[30] Yet amid this disgust with the military leaders, he did not quite abandon hope for the future: "I hope for a speedy death. To be conscripted and hit by a bullet. But when I think how hard it is to live, my fighting spirit springs forth."

Again and again, he returned to the cruelty of the Japanese leaders toward their own people: "Before the *gyokusai*, wounded soldiers in the Saipan hospital were given hand grenades. There were few prisoners. In the case of Iwo Jima, I gather that the medical officers poisoned the wounded."[31]

Unlike many Japanese diarists of the time, Watanabe had no sympathy for Hitler: "Hitler, Mussolini, Goebbels are all dead. What joy for suffering humanity! They were all monsters."[32]

He had difficulty deciding whether to remain in Tokyo. He wrote on June 1, "After the heavy air attack on the 25th, I intended to leave Tokyo for a while." But he then asked himself, "Do you plan to spend your days in idleness without necessary books? Will you be able to go on living without doing anything?" If he remained in Tokyo, he would be expected to go to weekly faculty meetings, though their only purpose was to expose the attendees to the danger of death. But, he decided, it was his duty to continue to live for the sake of his country, a country on the point of collapse that nevertheless must continue to exist: "I am nothing as an intellectual, but even the likes of me will surely be of service to the Japan of the future. This is because I detest and despise present-day Japan, which has committed a terrible mistake and is now making expiation."[33]

Watanabe continued to write his diary amid the air raids, even when tormented by uncertainties: "This little notebook must remain behind. It should be read by all Japanese, for here they will see the state of mind of a young Japanese who loved his country and humanity but who was ashamed of the way in which the country has behaved itself at so critical a moment."[34]

After considerable debate with himself, he left for the safety of Tsubame, the village in Niigata Prefecture to which his family had been evacuated. He was happy to be reunited with his family, but he felt that whatever he had achieved up until then counted for zero in Tsubame—or, for that matter, in Japan. Japan, surrounded by American military forces, was about to commit suicide:

> What point is there in preaching love for humanity and good will, for urging intellectual cooperation among the nations? What point is there in preaching repentance and redemption to people about to commit suicide?
>
> Our country must die. And then it must be reborn.
>
> Thousands and thousands of houses have been burned, set afire, destroyed. And men, women, children with them. The sky turns red in the night, pitch black in the day. The siege of Tokyo is beginning.
>
> This is the time when all Japanese must become truly aware of what war is, what militarism is, and what politics are when led by fanaticism.
>
> But, alas, total illumination comes slowly; in the provinces people still believe in final victory. May awakening come soon! May morning come soon![35]

At times, Watanabe may have felt exhausted by the weight of being a thinking man. Reading in the diary of Edmond de Goncourt the description of the siege of Paris in 1870, he commented that though the Parisians were starving, wounded, and trapped, they were far more fortunate than the Japanese of 1945. Goncourt loved his country and cursed defeatism among his friends, but toward the end of the siege he complained of "a feeling of weariness at being a Frenchman, and a vague desire to search for a country where an artist can think in peace, and not be disturbed incessantly by the stupid agitation and foolish convulsions of the destructive mass of people." Surely Goncourt's feelings were similar to Watanabe's sentiments at this stage of the war.

Watanabe related that a cousin had declared his intention of fighting to the end, even at the cost of his life. After all that had happened, the cousin said, the Japanese had no choice but to pursue the war to the bitter end. This cry from the heart struck Watanabe as representing the feelings of most Japanese. "Tragically stupid!" was his judgment. He added, "Such cries, when acted on, lead the country into nothingness."[36]

One of Watanabe's most outspoken pronouncements on the war was written at a time when Japanese soldiers were still resisting in the Ryukyu Islands:

Sooner or later, they will be defeated. What will the Americans do after taking these islands? What will we do? They will bomb us with ferocity, and we will resist with desperation. The militarists with the sacrosanct imperial power that they have arrogated are pushing us into murder and suicide.

I have been against the war from the start. This war is neither holy or just. It is nothing more than a dazzling stunt of our imperialistic capitalism, inevitably recognized as such by the capitalists and vaguely explained by the insensate militarists.[37]

Watanabe had no use for any of the "isms" of left or right, considering that they were all preposterous fictions projected by magic lanterns, lies that each country manufactured in order to justify its own position.

From beginning to end, he unceasingly opposed the war, but recognized that in one respect he himself had changed: "I, who before the war always feared and cursed the superficial enthusiasm for Americanism, just before the outbreak of war came to curse also the frightening xenophobia."[38]

The diary is filled with brilliant passages that cry out for quotation. Some relate to events reported in the newspapers, others refer to books Watanabe was reading, but most are his reflections on the suffering of Japan in the final agony of the war. One wonders what would have happened to Watanabe if a member of the military police who could read French had found this diary.

Itō Sei's reactions were less complex. His diary entry for March 10, the day of the worst aerial attack, is businesslike: "Most of Tokyo has now been turned into ashes. What will happen to those who have lost their homes? What will happen to those living on rations? And what effects will this have on those of us whose houses are in the suburbs?"[39]

Five days later, more like himself, Itō wrote,

> I gather that of late the militarists are saying that the enemy is certain to land, and that we can't win the war unless every last Japanese carries on guerrilla warfare. If that should happen, we will go into the mountains at Chichibu and in Kōshū and, keeping out of sight of enemy planes, lead a life of constant night attacks on enemy positions. This may seem a mere fantasy, in terms of our present lives, but such a day may come more quickly than we expect.[40]

THE AIR RAID of March 10, 1945, terrified the inhabitants of Tokyo, but even people living in towns that were not bombed shared the fright. Kamakura, where a considerable number of writers lived, buzzed with rumors of imminent landings by American troops, and the navy hastily constructed fortifications to block the anticipated invasion. Kamakura, as it turned out, was never attacked, but the inhabitants could not count on the Americans sparing the city in deference to its historic importance and magnificent temples.

Takami Jun, apprehensive about the safety of Kamakura, decided to send his mother back to the country. Ueno Station was filled with people desperately intent on escaping to somewhere that was less likely to be bombed. The sight brought back to Takami scenes that he had witnessed in China the previous year, and he compared the Chinese and Japanese. Chinese crowds tended to be noisy, shouting and raising a great commotion even when not as numerous as the crowd in Ueno Station. Takami was deeply affected by the difference between the clamorous Chinese and the quiet, courageous, patient, humble, composed Japanese:

> Before I knew it, tears had poured from my eyes. My heart was full of love and affection. I thought that I wanted to live with these people and die with them. No—though I was not the victim of a bombing, I was one with such people. These ordinary people have not been authorized to emit angry voices. They have no influence they can depend on, no money, but as they wait in patient silence they love and trust Japan from their hearts. I was one with them.[1]

Faced with the likely confiscation of his house by the military, Takami sent his most precious possessions—five volumes of his diary and a book of reproductions of Cézanne's paintings—to a safe place in the countryside. He had no choice but to sell other belongings—anything that might find a buyer—because the drying up of demand for his writings had left Takami without an income. When he heard that his friend, the critic Kobayashi Hideo (1902–1983), was planning to dispose of his possessions at an auction house in Itō, Takami asked Kobayashi to take with him some things he hoped to sell: a briefcase bought in Java, his wife's handbag, a crocodile-skin wallet, a Baldax camera, and several lengths of printed cloth from Java. He wondered if they would fetch even ¥2000.[2] Kobayashi, likewise in financial difficulty, sold part of his beloved collection of ceramics to an antiques dealer. Many people were eager to sell their possessions, and the dealers took advantage and beat down the prices. They also urged sellers to accept goods in place of cash as payment. Kobayashi left Itō with nothing but a splendid antique bowl.[3]

Takami heard that men were needed for work on cattle farms, and decided that if Kamakura became too dangerous, he would apply for a job at one of those farms. Just at this time, however, a more welcome possibility presented itself. The novelist Kume Masao (1891–1952) had decided to start a lending library in Kamakura. The war had deprived people of most entertainments, and they craved books. Kume planned to ask literary men living in Kamakura to lend books from their collections to the library, which in turn would lend them to readers on payment of a fee. The lenders would receive part of the fees charged for borrowing their books.

The Kamakura Library, as it came to be called, was a success. More than a hundred people became members on May 1, 1945, the day it opened for business. The cheerful entry in Takami's diary describing the events of that day concluded, however, with a series of troubling dispatches from abroad. The first, from Zurich, reported that Benito Mussolini had been arrested. The second, from Shanghai, declared that Germany had capitulated, but the third, from Lisbon, denied the rumor. A dispatch on the following day from Stockholm reported that a radio broadcast from Berlin had concluded with a quotation from Frederick the Great: "If the end should come, I will accept it with honor." The words doubtless conveyed the final resolve of the Führer.[4]

On May 3, Adolf Hitler's death was officially announced. Berlin fell two days later, and Germany surrendered on May 8. Takami wrote,

Germany has at last been defeated. Nobody has anything special to say about this major event; no doubt people feel that a day that was fated to come has at last arrived. They don't even treat it as anything of exceptional importance. This, when one thinks of it, is peculiar.

We have experienced one crisis after another until our nerves have become insensitive to the point of numbness. That may be part of the explanation. When one's own house is in danger, one can't worry about a fire on the opposite shore of the river. Also, I never could get to like Hitler. I often reproached myself, thinking I had perhaps fallen victim to British-American strategic propaganda, but I had a uneasy dislike of the Nazis. This feeling seems not to have been confined to myself. Most people probably felt the same. That may be why, even when they heard that Germany had finally fallen, they felt neither sympathy nor distress. But I feel sorry for the German people.[5]

Yamada Fūtarō, on learning of Hitler's death, expressed his admiration for the fallen hero:

Of late, many great stars have fallen. Hitler's death was not unexpected, but it could not fail to make an inexpressibly profound impression on us. He was truly a hero.

However present-day histories may judge him, he was a titan of human history, worthy to rank with Caesar, Charles XII, Napoléon, Alexander, Peter the Great. When we think of him, when we realize that we lived under the same sky with him, we cannot but conclude, unable to suppress a strange excitement, that the present ranks as a historic age and deserves a special place in the long history of the world as a heroic age, a tempestuous age, a terrifying age, a glorious age.[6]

Neither Takami nor Yamada noted that Japan, having lost its two major allies, was left virtually alone to fight the rest of the world. But, discussing a newspaper report on the fighting in Borneo, Takami wrote on May 11:

We are clearly being pushed back by the enemy. We are losing. Why can't they write this plainly? Why can't they write it plainly and appeal to the people? It's the same old story. That's why people are not taken in by reassuring, deceptive articles. They have learned to read between the lines. What necessity is there for the newspapers to print such articles?[7]

The loss of Iwo Jima, after a prolonged and desperate struggle, was the last battle to move the diarists emotionally. Takami had written on March 21, the day he heard the news:

This afternoon at three, there was an announcement of the *gyoku-sai* on Iwo Jima. The voice of the announcer as he read the text of Commanding Officer Kuribayashi [Tadamichi]'s radio message was choked with tears. I felt a lump rise in my throat. When I thought of the men who have died on Iwo Jima, swallowing their bitter feelings, I felt somehow ashamed to live on, doing nothing.[8]

Yamada Fūtarō expressed no personal reaction to news of the American landing on Iwo Jima, but noted,

By air, it is a bare three hours from the Imperial Palace. The newspapers are extremely lugubrious in describing how vital to us this little island in the Pacific is. A huge enemy task force of 300 ships is still cruising around the island as if the waters separating it from the main islands were their own little pond. Are we going to lose this island, like the others? Tokyo will be exposed, literally day in and day out, to enemy bombers. The present situation is so desperate that nobody would think it absurd if it were reported the enemy had begun landing on the Bōsō shore.[9]

The ongoing battle for the Philippines had hardly ended before the even more crucial battle for Okinawa began. The press and the popular magazines exerted every effort to convince readers that the fighting on Okinawa provided the Japanese forces with a superb opportunity to destroy once and for all the American menace, but confidence in Japan's certain victory rapidly waned. Reading diaries dating from the period after the American landing on Okinawa in April 1, 1945, one is likely to be surprised at how seldom the fighting is mentioned. No doubt, as Takami said, people had been dazed by the innumerable crises, each demanding their attention. Whenever some island was invaded, the newspapers invariably declared that the outcome of the battle was crucial to Japan's survival, but the conclusion was always the same: despite the heroic efforts of the defenders, the island had fallen to the Americans.

The diarists were at first optimistic about the progress of the fighting on and around Okinawa. On April 18, Yamada wrote that 393 enemy warships had been sunk or damaged in the area of Okinawa, and he predicted that the attack on Okinawa would soon end in tragedy for the Americans. He went on, "However, the enemy fleet, still obstinately refusing to quit nearby waters, continues its bombardment. All our planes are being used for special attack. The shape of the ultimate battle between Japan and America has begun to reveal itself in the battle for Okinawa. It is too horrible for words."[10]

On May 12, the *Yomiuri shinbun* reported another naval victory. Seventeen warships, including aircraft carriers, had been sunk or damaged. The enemy, the article prophesied, would be unable to make up these losses. Japanese forces were urged not to relent in their pursuit of fleeing enemy ships. Such a wonderful chance of total victory might never come again.[11]

Tokutomi Sohō, one of the most vocal exponents of the war, published a long article on May 14 in the *Mainichi shinbun* enumerating Japanese successes. He claimed that between April 6 and May 4, the Special Attack Force had destroyed or badly damaged one-third of the 1400 American warships that participated in the battle for Okinawa. He called for the Japanese to replace the ships they had lost with twice as many so they could not only drive the Americans from Okinawa but recapture Iwo Jima and Saipan. He added, "This is not merely a question of one island, Okinawa. The fate of the nation depends on it. If we lose Okinawa, our lifeline to the south will be severed, and it will provide the enemy with a base from which to attack the main Japanese islands."[12]

Four days after Tokutomi's article describing Japanese successes appeared, Takami wrote in his diary that Okinawa was in danger. "I had thought there was nothing to worry about," he wrote in dismay. The newspapers now agreed that the situation was critical. The *Mainichi shinbun* declared that a land victory on Okinawa was essential; it was premature to suppose that Japan enjoyed an advantage because its navy had sunk so many enemy warships. An all-out land attack was the only way to victory.[13]

Not everyone believed that the survival of Japan hung on the outcome of the fighting on Okinawa. The writer Unno Jūza, though a strong supporter of the war, was annoyed by accounts in the press that likened the battle for Okinawa to Tennōzan and Sekigahara, sites of the most critical battles of Japanese history. He wrote in his diary on July 14, soon after the defeat on Okinawa,

> Was the battle for Okinawa actually a Tennōzan or a Sekigahara? It will take some time before this is decided, but I can say quite definitely that I am not much impressed by the comparisons. It may have been necessary to use such far-fetched expressions in order to build up the people's fighting strength and their hatred of the enemy; but if, now that Okinawa has fallen, people become prey to despair, supposing that continuing the fight is useless, that Japan is finished, they will be incapable of action. This would create a grave problem.
>
> Okinawa was no Tennōzan or Sekigahara. It wasn't that important.[14]

As usual, rumors often took the place of news. The number of American warships sunk by the Special Attack Force, as given by Yamada Fūtarō and Tokutomi Sohō, was enormously inflated; the American fleet, despite some losses, was largely intact. Rumors were not always encouraging. On May 28, Itō Sei wrote, "Just as I heard in rumors, the Imperial Palace has burned. Tokyo Station has burned. The Ginza has been completely destroyed. Places like Azabu and Akasaka that had hitherto survived the bombing have now burned to the ground. I hear that the Greater East Asia Ministry has burned. People say that Tokyo doesn't exist any more." Itō followed this discouraging report, however, with a hopeful new rumor:

> Yesterday I met Momota on the street. He told me something amazing—that the enemy on Okinawa had unconditionally surrendered. Students he met on the way were ecstatic. He said, "If this is true, nothing could make me happier, even though I've

been burned out." After he went off, I asked some other people. They said they had come here today by foot from the Nakano area, and that the rumor was true. Everywhere they went, people were shouting "Banzai!" and putting out flags. When I passed by the military police, I asked about the rumor. They said they had no definite word, but it might be true. I felt my heart pound at the thought. But I also thought that now, when Tokyo has been completely reduced to ashes, the rumor might be the work of the enemy intelligence network, or it might be a wishful dream of the people. If that was how such a rumor came to be circulated in the city, it was truly a bad sign. The rumor started yesterday, but it was not confirmed last night, this morning, or evening on the radio. Tonight there was instead a report on the commendation given to over one hundred "human torpedo attack men." This was the first announcement that we have a Special Attack Force that makes use of rocket bombs, said to be a new weapon.

Itō's diary at this point mentions without comment the "false report" of an enemy surrender on Okinawa.[15] Numerous stories about spies were invented to explain the rumors and Japanese losses. Yamada Fūtarō gave some examples of "groundless rumors." One told of a spy who was an official in a certain ministry. Whenever there was an air raid, he would go down to the basement of his house and tap out wireless messages. His wife played the piano to muffle the sounds. He was unintentionally exposed by a school composition written by his young son.[16] The novelist Osaragi Jirō (1897–1973) gave the account of another spy case, prefacing it with a cautionary phrase:

This may be a false rumor, but there was a crazy woman who was often seen wandering around a factory in Tsuchiura with her mouth wide open. One day, she went inside the gate and was searched. She proved to be a nisei soldier disguised as a woman. Whether or not the story is true, it is a fact that the enemy is able in a short space of time to sniff out wherever a factory has been evacuated and then bomb it with precision.[17]

Diaries increasingly mentioned the propaganda leaflets dropped by American planes. Osaragi pasted into his diary a page of the June 1 issue of the *Mariana jihō* with the headline "Star-Spangled Banner Waves over Shuri Castle." A photograph shows Okinawan children playing with their new toy, a jeep. Another leaflet carried a picture of President Truman and his message declaring that the enemies of the Americans were the Japanese military and officials, and that the Americans had no intention of enslaving the Japanese people.[18]

Yamada saw a propaganda leaflet dropped by a B-29 on Tokyo in early June. One side showed a colored photograph of St. Luke's Hospital in Tokyo. The reverse identified the hospital as a gift from the United States to Japan. This was followed by a text:

The Japanese militarists attacked Pearl Harbor without obtaining the consent of His Majesty the Emperor.... Our enemies are the militarists, not you, the people.... We fully recognize your bravery, but the war is clearly going to your disadvantage. Further resistance will only increase the number of victims who die in vain. The American production of ships and planes is as different from Japan's as the sun is to the stars. If you persist in fighting, we will repeatedly and exhaustively bomb your cities until you are left with nothing. But we truly love peace. We have no desire to give ourselves to violence. People of Japan! Your happiness will begin when you lay down your swords. Then, when once again you are friends to America, as you were before the war, come with your hand outstretched in friendship. We will certainly not treat you unfairly. Etc.

Yamada's comment was, "Just as clever as one might expect, but they do not realize that the Japanese are convinced there can be no happiness after surrender."[19]

During the last stages of the war, American planes regularly dropped propaganda leaflets following a raid. The *Rakkasan nyūsu* (*Parachute News*), published in Manila, was in the form of a weekly newspaper. As many as 2 million copies were printed and scattered over Japan and in areas of Southeast Asia where there was fighting. Most of the articles were factual, but some were American propaganda, such as the claim that life in the relocation camps in the western United States was rather like a vacation for the interned Japanese Americans.[20] Presumably this was an attempt to rebut the Japanese assertion that the "relocation" of Japanese Americans was an example of American racial prejudice. It has been estimated that about one-third of the Japanese who read the leaflets believed them.[21]

Once the Americans had taken Okinawa, their next move could only be the invasion of the main islands. Most of the major Japanese cities had been destroyed, and the B-29s, finding no new targets in Tokyo or Osaka, had turned their attention to medium-size towns. If the bombing continued, little would be left of any Japanese city. Yamada Fūtarō, on his way back to Tokyo from his home on the Japan Sea coast, changed trains at Kyoto. The day spent there brought reflections on the fate of a city that, more than any other, embodied the Japanese past:

> The destruction of Kyoto is imminent. During the last two months and even within the last ten days, one has come to envision, almost with certainty, its transformation into ruins. What must people living in Kyoto feel? Osaka, which is within hailing distance, has already been completely destroyed. The people of Kyoto, of course, are afraid, but they seem incapable of imagining destruction without having first physically experienced the pain. Even the air-raid shelters along the streets are dainty in the Kyoto manner, and the evacuation of buildings is in the nature of child's play.
>
> I gather there were whispers on the reason why Yokohama was not bombed even once, even as Tokyo was being reduced to ashes. They asserted it was because the Americans were so attached to a place where they had once done business that they could not bomb either the city or the harbor. But one day, 600 planes carried out a fierce attack, and in an instant Yokohama was wiped out.

We who live in Tokyo, if for three days enemy planes fail to pay a visit, tend to forget about the air raids, as if they occurred in the distant past.... I wonder if the people of Kyoto, fearful and resolute by turns, are not hoping that the Americans will spare the old capital, known to tourists throughout the world. If one asked, they would deny it, but at the bottom of their hearts are they not clinging to this last ray of reassurance? It is dangerous.

But when I looked at the lovely old capital smoldering in the rain, I did not feel in the least the self-satisfaction of the prophet of doom. My heart was filled with grief. I wished I could save Kyoto. It will be simple to rebuild cities like Tokyo or Osaka that are no more than conglomerations of rubbish, haphazardly thrown together. A new Tokyo could possess the dignity of the capital of an empire, and a new Osaka could look in every way a capital of commerce. But once Kyoto is lost, it can never be restored; this city is a symbol of the past. It cannot be re-created any more than one's childhood from an album of photographs. Would a rebuilt Kinkaku or Ginkaku be a true Kinkaku or Ginkaku?[22]

Takami Jun's nostalgia was directed at Asakusa, a tawdry but lively section of Tokyo, known before the war for its entertainments, including prostitution. Many of Takami's prewar works were set in Asakusa, and even Kawabata Yasunari (1899–1972), celebrated for his evocations of traditional culture, had evoked in several novels the atmosphere of Asakusa. The fact that the Sensōji, the biggest and best-known temple in Asakusa, had escaped harm during the Great Kantō Earthquake of 1923 was taken as proof of the miraculous powers of the enshrined deity Kannon. But when Takami walked through the neighborhood on March 12, just after the devastating air raid two days earlier, the temple had vanished and almost nothing else was left of Asakusa:

My beloved Asakusa. That Asakusa which holds a mysterious charm for me. I grew up in the Yamanote section of the city, but I had an affection for Asakusa that I cannot describe in words, the

Asakusa that inspired such love in me. That Asakusa disappeared one morning. I suppose it will be rebuilt some day, but I am sure its old appearance can never be restored. They can only build an entirely different Asakusa. That hugger-mugger, effervescent Asakusa. That Asakusa—dirty, squalid, and for that reason lovable, with its inexplicable charm—is no more. Probably, it is gone forever. The Kannon that survived even the earthquake burned this time. Many people took refuge here, supposing Kannon would keep them safe this time, too, but they burned to death, perishing in the flames of the main temple building. Objects that looked like their corpses were piled up here and there behind the temple ruins. Some were so small that they no doubt were children.[23]

Nagai Kafū, who for most of the war had treated it mainly as a great inconvenience imposed on him by the military, learned what war is like when his home, the Henkikan, was incinerated. He wandered from one temporary lodging to another, only to be burned out three times. He now suffered not merely from a scarcity of Lipton tea but from real deprivation. On May 1, he noted in his diary that there was no longer any running water in his rooming house. Gas had been cut off ever since the raid on April 15: "Every day I burn scraps of wood taken from destroyed houses to cook my meals. Life in a defeated country—no water, no fire. One can fairly say that we have reached the extreme of misery."[24]

For him, Japan was already defeated. When he went to the tax office to apply, as a disaster victim, for exemption from taxes, the procedures were so complicated that he gave up. No one offered to help. He seemed to have lost his identity as a famous author. Everything irritated him, but the main object of Kafū's hatred remained the military police, not the Americans: "Ever since the streets of Tokyo were turned into scorched earth, anyone who dares to discuss the future course of the war is dragged off by the military police. They also censor the mail, and a great many people have been punished."[25]

Much of what Kafū recorded in his diary was mere hearsay. He could not resist mentioning that a fortune-teller living near Yutenji in

Meguro had predicted a sudden Japanese victory in June. Rumors circulated in Sasazuka that Jizō, the guardian deity of children, had uttered the same prediction.

The war showed no signs of abating in June, though there were fewer air attacks on Tokyo. Kafū left Tokyo on June 2 with friends, expecting to take refuge from the bombing at their old home in Akashi, not far from Kōbe. When they arrived, however, they discovered that the house was jammed with refugees and there was no room for anyone else. They moved on to Okayama, arriving just in time for an air raid.

Kafū at this time wrote to Tanizaki Jun'ichirō (1886–1965), his former disciple, who had taken refuge in Katsuyama, a small town in the mountains. Tanizaki responded with a gift of necessary articles, including scissors, a pocket knife, a thousand sheets of manuscript paper, a bathrobe, and a sash. "I couldn't keep back the tears of gratitude," Kafū wrote.[26]

Kafū was shown an American propaganda leaflet that someone had picked up in Osaka. It opened "Great men of Japan! Where are you?" The leaflet, citing by name the titans of the Meiji era who had fought for freedom, insisted that the only way to ensure the future of Japan was by establishing once again freedom of speech and a democratic government.[27] Kafū made no comment.

On August 10, Kafū reported in his diary that news of the total destruction of Hiroshima had caused panic among the inhabitants of Okayama. He decided at this point to pay Tanizaki a visit.

Kafū made his way to Okayama Station along dark streets lit only by the morning star. The station was already crowded with people hoping to buy tickets. Some had spent the night waiting outside the station. There was such a crowd that Kafū all but abandoned the trip to Katsuyama. He managed to pull himself together and take his place at the end of the line. Even after he succeeded in getting a ticket, there was a long wait before the train departed, but Kafū gradually began to enjoy the journey. He conversed with an old woman seated opposite him, and when she opened her lunch box, she gave him part of the contents—potatoes, flour, and pumpkins mashed together. To his surprise, he found that it tasted quite good.

On reaching Katsuyama, he went to the house where Tanizaki was living. Tanizaki used the second floor for his study, but shared the ground floor with a large number of evacuated relatives. Kafū was introduced to Tanizaki's wife, "a slender, beautiful woman." Tanizaki told him that he had planned to have Kafū stay at an inn with a fine view, but the building had been requisitioned for German detainees, who were no longer allies. Kafū stayed at a modest inn, but the food was the best he had eaten in a long time. The rice was provided by Tanizaki.

The next morning, Tanizaki showed his guest around the town, and Kafū had lunch in Tanizaki's lodgings. Tanizaki urged Kafū to remain in Katsuyama. Kafū was tempted, but in the end he that decided he could not impose any further on Tanizaki at a time of a severe food shortage.[28] That evening, Tanizaki sent a messenger inviting Kafū to dinner. The food was good, and the saké was delicious. Mrs. Tanizaki became slightly tipsy, helping to make the conversation enjoyable. Kafū left at nine o'clock, apologizing for staying too long. Although he did not say so, he probably felt that the Tanizakis lived in a different world from the one in which he lived.

The next morning, August 15, breakfast at the inn consisted of eggs, miso soup, dace broiled in soy, and eggplant pickled in saké lees. Kafū felt as if he were eating a meal at the finest restaurant in Tokyo. He went to Tanizaki's house to say good-bye. Tanizaki had managed to buy a ticket for him to Okayama. On the train Kafū, ate the lunch that Mrs. Tanizaki had packed for him. It was so delicious that he felt indescribable joy.

When Kafū returned to his lodgings in Okayama, his friends asked, "Haven't you heard? The radio broadcast at noon today announced that the war between Japan and America has suddenly ended." Kafū wrote in his diary, "That was fine with me." That evening, he and his friends had a feast to celebrate the end of the fighting.[29]

Kafū responded with incredible equanimity to the news that the war was over. He may have thought of peace mainly in terms of a restoration of his prewar life, when a meal with white rice did not bring tears of gratitude. The war had made him a beggar, thankful for whatever scraps of food he was given. He hated those who had brought this about, and when he learned of the defeat, he celebrated.

There could hardly been a greater contrast between Kafū's reactions and Yamada Fūtarō's. Yamada wrote in his diary on August 14:

> Japan is standing at the last line of defense. It is being driven over a precipice where pitch-black storm winds howl. One step farther, and we'll drop into a hell of destruction.
>
> The American forces that grabbed Iwo Jima and massacred Okinawa send thousands of planes night and day without let-up, and a huge fleet is cruising in nearby waters, ready to bombard, strafe, and shell, again and again. Most of our cities have been reduced to ruins. Innumerable people have fled to the countryside, and on top of everything else, the enemy has invented a terrifying atomic bomb that in one instant wiped out Hiroshima.
>
> The phoenix-like Soviet Union, which annihilated Germany, our only ally, on August 8 finally declared war on Japan. And we have spent eight years in hard fighting with that monster, the Chinese people. Can Japan, hacked all over with wounds, still confront America and Britain and do battle against the entire world?[30]

On August 12, Itō Sei conceded that his fatherland was in its last extremity, under attack from air and sea, but he remained confident that the fighting would continue for a long time: "The Yamato race, regardless of the circumstances, will fight on as long as it can fight. However, our capability, our ultimate capability, is not known to either our people or the enemy. I believe we still have the strength to fight a good deal more."[31]

Osaragi Jirō heard from a friend on August 11 that the government had replied through the Swiss and Swedish ministers that it was willing to accept the terms of the Potsdam Declaration, providing it was understood that the Imperial Institution would remain unaltered. Osaragi commented,

This, in other words, is unconditional surrender. This can only mean that the militarists, having deceived the people with lie piled on lie, have at last thrown in the towel. A painful moment unexampled in our history has come, and yet people can't help but feel somehow relieved and reassured! Acts committed in the dark that were both base and arrogant have brought this about.[32]

Unno Jūza, on hearing that the Red Army had crossed the borders of Manchukuo and Korea on August 9, felt giddy, sure that nothing worse could have happened. Despite the vehemently anti-Communist stance of Japan, the government had believed that the Soviet Union, because of the Soviet-Japanese Neutrality Pact of 1941, would mediate an end to the war. Even after the Soviet Union announced that it would not renew the treaty, Japan did not abandon this hope. It was clear to Unno that there was no chance left of a peaceful solution to the war, let alone a Japanese victory. He wrote,

My family!

After we have died, will Japan perish or will it prosper? It will be one or the other. If it thrives, it will give us the greatest possible satisfaction. Even if it perishes, surely someone of a future generation will take up the pure and noble remains of the 2600 years of our people, and this will bring recovery and resurgence. They may then welcome us who dwell in the world of the dead to a pure and peaceful shrine.

At this juncture of time, I am resolved not to die an ignominious death and be laughed at by people of the future.

Spirits of my ancestors! Come above us, join our battle, protect us! Give us, a family of seven, boundless and inexhaustible strength![33]

Like many other Japanese, Unno could not imagine living in a defeated Japan. He was prepared to die and to take his family with him.

6

ON APRIL 5, 1945, the Soviet Union informed Japan that it had renounced the Soviet-Japanese Neutrality Pact, signed in April 1941. The treaty, like the Soviet-German Non-Aggression Pact of 1939, had astonished all who were aware of the intense hostility the signatories had long displayed toward each other. Japan had concluded the Anti-Comintern Pact with Germany in 1936 and the Tripartite Pact with Germany and Italy in 1940, both intended to combat the Communist International. The Soviet Union, in turn, had branded Japan as an aggressor. In 1939, Soviet and Japanese forces bitterly clashed at Nomonhan on the frontier between Mongolia and Japanese-held Manchukuo.

It seemed unthinkable that two such antagonists could reach agreement on any issue, but the Soviet-Japanese Neutrality Pact was in fact mutually beneficial, satisfying the desire of both countries to maintain a peaceful frontier at a time when their troops were needed elsewhere. In the summer of 1945, when Japan stood alone and many in the government (and even in the military) hoped for a negotiated termination of the war, the existence of the neutrality pact led them to believe that the Soviet Union might mediate between Japan and the Allies.[1]

The Japanese were suddenly at pains to avoid offending the sole possible mediator. The newspapers, in a startling change of attitude, began to publish favorable articles about the Soviet Union. The new position extended beyond the press. Filmmakers were ordered not to include anything in their scripts that might offend the Russians, even a mention of the Russo-Japanese War.[2]

The Postdam Declaration of July 26, 1945, signed by the United States, Great Britain, and China, announced the Allies' intention of causing the "prompt and utter destruction" of Japan unless it surrendered unconditionally. The Soviet Union, still technically bound by the neutrality treaty,[3] did not sign the declaration. This bolstered Japanese hopes of Soviet mediation, but these hopes were dashed when the Soviet Union declared war on Japan on August 8, two days after the first atomic bomb was dropped on Hiroshima. Soviet troops crossed the borders into Manchukuo and Korea the next day.

The Japanese press at first made only brief references to the "new variety" of bomb and did not mention the violation of Japanese territory. The press was muzzled, and important news was often transmitted mainly by word of mouth. On August 9, Hayashi Fusao (1903–1975), a former leftist whose political views had swung to the extreme right, visited the office of the Kamakura Library. He announced, "We're in a real mess. We've lost the war." Takami Jun assumed that he was referring to the bombing of Hiroshima, but Hayashi said, "You haven't heard? The Soviet Union has declared war." Later that day, the novelist Nagai Tatsuo (1904–1980), visiting the library, reported that Nagasaki had been attacked with an atomic bomb. The damage was said to be worse than that at Hiroshima. Takami noted, "He had this from both

Dōmei and Asahi reporters, so it doesn't seem to be just a false rumor."[4]

On the following day, August 10, the newspapers at last mentioned the Soviet declaration of war, but said nothing about the bomb that had blasted Nagasaki. The *Yomiuri shinbun* gave greatest prominence to a report on the Tōgūshoku, an office created within the Imperial Household Ministry to administer matters concerning the young crown prince. The appointment of a new tutor to the crown prince also received detailed attention. Takami wrote,

> We were taken completely by surprise by the Soviet declaration of war. Perhaps people on the inside foresaw it, but we knew nothing. We had instead been secretly hoping that the Soviet Union would mediate. Everybody had the same thought. The attitude displayed toward the Soviet Union in newspaper articles was adulatory. And then, all of a sudden, came the Soviet declaration of war. . . .
>
> The radio says nothing about the question of the Soviet Union or how the fighting with them is going. Instead, it keeps repeating news about the Tōgūshoku—that and nothing else. It has not yet been announced that Japan has declared war on the Soviet Union. What a weird day this has been![5]

Later on, a customer came to the library with the news that there had been a conference of high-ranking officials in the presence of His Majesty and that they had decided to request an armistice. Takami wrote,

> I felt somehow in a daze even though the conclusion of the war, which I had so desperately hoped for, seemed about to materialize. I had always imagined how happy I would be when this occurred, but in fact I didn't feel any great excitement. Was it because I didn't trust what that customer had said? All the same, the war will soon come to a close. Conclude with a miserable defeat—Is that why I felt so downcast?[6]

The radio reported that Minister of the Army Anami Korechika had declared that Japan would fight to the finish. Takami commented, "In that case, everybody will be mobilized, and everybody will get killed. The country and the people will all perish."[7]

He described his train journey back home from the library:

> People were quite composed, on both the train and the platforms. Was this true composure? Or had despondency brought on a feeling of "Whatever happens, there's nothing we can do about it"? . . . Not one person mentioned the Soviet declaration of war. Nobody was excited. Nobody lamented. Nobody was upset. But I am sure that in their homes, where there was no danger of being overheard, they had a good deal to say. Keeping our mouths shut when we're in public has been our prime consideration. If one just happens to say something ill-advised and then gets arrested, it's nothing to laugh at. That's why they're silent. It's the politics of terror. . . . If that's what's kept people silent, it proves we could never have won the war. Who drove the people into such a state?[8]

On August 11, the top article in both the *Mainichi* and *Yomiuri* newspapers displayed a photograph of the crown prince with praise for his virtues. The newspapers mentioned also that the head of the Cabinet Information Bureau had voiced the government's determination to maintain the *kokutai*.[9]

The term *kokutai*, usually translated as "national polity," often appeared in discussions of the destiny of Japan published in the 1930s and 1940s; it was used in various senses but especially to convey the belief, which was not subject to argumentation, that Japan must retain at all costs the imperial institution. Takami guessed that the use of the term at this time might mask a decision to ask for an armistice. He blamed the calamitous state into which the country had fallen on the insistence of the military clique on the absolute importance of the *kokutai*:

We've undergone extreme indoctrination, and we feel it. At the same time, the expression on people's faces is one of profound resignation, seeming to say, "It doesn't matter what happens—no matter what happens, it can't be helped." It is not, however, the blackness of despair. It is without expression. Or, one might say, it is a colorless, tasteless, odorless expression of the belief "things will work out somehow."

This is the end. The feeling is deep-seated. There's no getting around it—we are exhausted, worn out physically and mentally. Not only our bodies but our spirits are at their twilight.[10]

Rumor had it that the Americans had replied to Japanese insistence on retaining the *kokutai*: "You're the defeated country, aren't you? Surrender has to be unconditional. You speak of preserving the *kokutai*, but wasn't the emperor your supreme leader during the war? And yet you tell us we mustn't touch him. The gall of you!"[11]

To add to the worries of the people of Tokyo, a rumor circulated that an atomic bomb would be dropped on Tokyo on August 13. The day passed without major incident, but alarm was raised on August 14 by the appearance of a single American plane. In the past, people had assumed that one plane was nothing to worry about; it was probably merely on reconnaissance. But after the experience of one plane over Hiroshima, a single plane seemed more dangerous than a squadron.

Takami noted that the newspapers, which had hitherto referred to the atomic bombs vaguely as "new-model bombs," had begun to call them by their real name. There were rumors afloat that the newspapers had been freed of the gag controls that had compelled them to print only what the authorities allowed. Takami commented, "When I think of it, the newspapers also bear responsibility for the defeat. One can't blame only the controls. Writers and intellectuals are also responsible. The defeat was not caused solely by the atomic bombs. We were defeated long before. The atomic bombs did nothing more than administer the coup de grâce."[12]

On the night of August 14, Takami, eager for more information than the newspapers reported, went to see a friend, a newspaper man, who told him privately that there would be an announcement at eleven o'clock stating that the terms of the Potsdam Declaration had been accepted. The war was over! But all anyone could do was sigh. Takami recalled that people had often predicted that when the war ended they would run around the Ginza shouting, "Banzai! Banzai!" He had also supposed that he would go to the Ginza, shake hands with and embrace utter strangers, but the Ginza that night was dark and empty.[13]

Unbeknownst to Takami or other civilians, there was turmoil at the highest level of the Japanese government on the night of August 14. Earlier that day, the emperor, at the cabinet meeting he had summoned, declared that, being unable to tolerate the slaughter of more Japanese by prolonging the war, he favored acceptance of the terms of the Potsdam Declaration. He directly pleaded with Minister of the Army Anami to assent, though he knew that Anami favored prolongation of the war.[14] Anami, after wavering, in the end could not refuse the emperor. That night, the emperor recorded a speech accepting the terms imposed on Japan by the declaration. It was scheduled to be broadcast on the radio at noon on August 15. Anami prepared to commit seppuku (ritual disembowelment).

Even while the emperor was recording his announcement, a group of army officers was persuading members of the Imperial Guard to participate in a coup d'état. The rebels occupied the Imperial Palace and almost succeeded in capturing the emperor's recording and broadcasting instead a call for continued hostilities. The carefully hidden recording was saved, and on the morning of August 15 the radio newscasters, announcing that there would be an important broadcast at noon, commanded all Japanese to listen.[15]

That morning, a friend told Yamada Fūtarō that the emperor was to make a broadcast. He wrote,

At that instant the word "surrender?" flashed through my head, but I at once firmly suppressed the thought. See how peaceful Japan is today! Isn't the sky shining beautifully?

While I was listening to Professor Hirota lecture on dermatology at the Maruyama Public School, a piece of paper was circulated in the classroom asking which we thought the most likely content of the broadcast—Armistice? Surrender? Declaration of War? I unhesitatingly drew a circle above "Declaration of War." . . .

The broadcast was an extraordinary event, the first in history. Word that the emperor himself would make the announcement convinced me all the more that it would be an Imperial Declaration of War on the Soviet Union. In other words, on top of the fierce and terrible war we have been waging with America and Britain, we would be taking on a new enemy, the powerful Soviet Union. This indescribable national crisis would probably result in a hundred more times suffering than what the Japanese people have already endured. It was definitely not strange or inappropriate for the emperor himself at such a time to address the people and command them to make even greater efforts. If the emperor uttered the words "Fight to the last soldier!" surely every Japanese, with shouts of joy, would fight as the emperor asked, to the last soldier.

Yamada added, "Everybody, teachers and students alike, was absolutely certain that the Imperial Command would be a declaration of war on the Soviet Union."[16]

Radio reception of the emperor's broadcast was poor, and the words themselves were archaic and difficult to understand. Yamada wrote, "What a heartrending voice that was! Never in all my life have I heard a human voice so choked with blood and tears." But not all those who understood the broadcast could at first absorb the fact that Japan had lost the war.

I heard the broadcast on the island of Guam. Word had been received that there was to be an important broadcast from Tokyo, and I was asked to interpret. Fearing that I might not understand it, I took with me three intellectual prisoners of war. This was fortunate: I could hardly understand anything the emperor said, but when the broadcast ended I saw that the prisoners were weeping and knew what that meant.

The account in the diary of the popular radio commentator To-kugawa Musei (1894–1971) on hearing the "jade voice," is particularly moving:

The sound of a gong announced it was noon.

—A broadcast vouchsafed by His Majesty, the Emperor, will follow. Please listen respectfully.

—Stand!

At the command, we stood at attention on the tatami.

Next the music of "Kimi ga yo" issued forth from the radio. I doubt that in all the years since the national anthem was first composed it has ever been played at so sad a time. The melody, like a great wave of sadness, engulfed my whole body.

The melody ended. I felt increasingly tense.

The jade voice began to be audible.

The physical sensation when I heard his voice for the first time. Every cell in my body shook. . . .

What a pure voice it was!

A feeling of gratitude soaked through to the tips of my hair.

"Kimi ga yo" was played again.

The tears continued to drip down to the tatami at my feet, each making a plop.

In a sense, I am one of the most intractable of His Majesty's subjects. And yet that's the state I was in.

No doubt every household, every school, every company, every factory, every government office, every army barracks in Japan heard this broadcast, all in equal stillness. I wonder if there will ever again be in the world a monarch like this one, a people like this one?

So lovely a country will never perish! That's what I felt instinctively.

Just supposing, one chance in a million, it actually perishes, I will still rejoice that I had the privilege of being born in this country, rather than any other country in the world, in this, of all periods of mankind.

The time when Japan perishes will be the time when the beautiful history of mankind perishes! All that will be left afterward is the arid history of materialism. . . .

In the hour of defeat, what a blessing for Japan to have had this emperor! I believe that among all the emperors of history, not one had as fine a character as he. . . .

The present emperor is not what is called a hero. It goes without saying that he is not militaristic. He is a benevolent ruler, a man of great kindness and beauty of character.

During the reign of this benevolent monarch, Japan lost a war to a materialistic country that used the atomic bomb. . . .

It was for the best. The Japanese people in recent times have known only victory. The Japanese, for the first time, have been taught what it means to be completely defeated in a war fought with modern weapons. Sometimes one loses; sometimes one wins. A people that has not experienced both victory and defeat is still immature. Let us consider that we have at last come of age.[17]

The account of the emperor's broadcast in the diary of Princess Nashimoto Itsuko (1882–1976) shows no less gratitude toward the emperor, but she wrote with pride and anger:

At noon I was seated formally before the radio when "Kimi ga yo" sounded. Next, a voice announced that His Majesty would now speak. His Majesty delivered the rescript in his normal voice. He related that for four years we have fought America, Britain, and China, but the tide of war has gradually turned against us. In addition, of late America, resorting to despicable tactics, has used a new type of weapon against Hiroshima and Nagasaki. They have killed many people and destroyed their homes. "We are unable to endure the loss of any more of Our subjects, and if We were to lose the *kokutai*, which goes back three thousand years, We would have no excuse to offer Our ancestors. For this reason, We have decided to ask for peace and accept the

Potsdam Declaration, enduring whatever hardships may result, no matter how difficult to endure. We ask you, Our children, harkening to Our resolution, to endure."

Such was the gist of His words. As I listened, I felt a choking in my breast and, imagining what must be passing through His Majesty's mind, I felt pain. My prevailing emotion was deep gratitude to His Majesty for wishing to save His subjects, though He himself will have to endure innumerable afflictions. The tears welled up. An intolerable stain has besmirched the three thousand years of Japan's shining glory. But it would be worse to be devastated like Berlin. The enemy has not yet set foot on Japanese soil. Japan will not remain forever destroyed.

I feel a vexation I cannot fully express in words. A feeling of helplessness—it's all over. We shall become the little Japan of the past. We must develop science and make Japan a worthier country than ever. If the people, in response to His Majesty's awe-inspiring resolution, do not exert their energies to the utmost and strive for the prosperity of our country, there will be no forgiveness.

There are no words to express how truly are to be pitied the officers and men of our armed forces who during these four years offered up their lives to continue the fight, not to mention the many who died or were wounded in the war. And there are those whose houses burned in the air raids, parents and children who are separated, the bitterness of all who have had tragic experiences. As I have said many times, I wished that before the war ended we could, even once, make those living on the American mainland taste our pain. Unless the people of America and England suffer this pain, administered with all the powerful strength of the gods, my bitterness will not be eased. This bitterness must somehow be assuaged.[18]

The craving for vengeance voiced by the princess is seldom expressed openly in other diaries, but many shared her regret that Japan, deprived of Korea, Taiwan, and Manchukuo, would again be "little."

The emotions expressed by Hirabayashi Taiko (1905–1972) are quite the opposite of those of Princess Itsuko—not surprising, considering that her life had been marked by poverty and she had been a Communist. For Hirabayashi, as for others of her background, the end of the war brought liberation. At the time she was writing her diary, she was living in her hometown in the country, to where she had been evacuated from Tokyo. The following excerpts are from her diary for August 15:

Air-raid alarms from early this morning inform us that a task force is about to attack. Is their purpose simply to reduce us to exhaustion? If an American landing is inevitable, I hope they land very soon. This must surely be the hope of almost every Japanese, worn out by excessive irritation.

Yesterday I heard (among other reports) that there will be a radio broadcast by the emperor on the following day. This is something unprecedented. My mother and I discussed whether it was more likely to be an announcement of surrender or a call for further resistance. We tried thinking it over, but to no avail. One could imagine that if it is decided to continue resistance, it might be necessary to have the emperor play a role; and if it is a surrender, that of course would be true. In the end, my mother, though she worries about her son on the battlefront, spoke as if she was resigned to the broadcast being a call for continuation of the war. For some days, it has been my mother's opinion that, since there's no chance of winning the war, a quick surrender would be best for both sides.

Noon arrived. . . . All the neighbors had gathered with unusually tense expressions on their faces. The radio, following a solemn announcement, played "Kimi ga yo." The long-drawn-out notes sounded particularly drawn-out today. Presently the emperor's voice could be heard in what sounded like a recording. The radio waves were distorted by all the mountains they had crossed, and there was a great deal of static. It was almost impossible to understand the words. . . . But at breaks in the noise we caught the words "acceptance of the Potsdam Declaration." The words "surrender" and "defeat" were avoided, but I knew this meant unconditional surrender.

I had been mentally prepared to accept that this was not impossible, but it took my breath away. Outside, people went by in the heat, as if depicted in an oil painting, mountainous bundles of hay on their backs. It's ended at last. It's ended. The war, like everything else, has ended. It's ended.

I felt like jumping up and shouting something a hundred times to the sky. I wanted to think I had been set free, but, perhaps because the bonds were so tight and so strong, I could not immediately feel a sense of liberation.

My neighbors, who knew nothing about the Potsdam Declaration, hearing my explanation that it meant unconditional surrender, for the first time burst into tears. The old woman, my neighbor from the house in front, came running up with a rag in one hand that she used to wipe away the tears. Weeping and sobbing, she said she was ready to die at any time. . . .

At night we removed the blackout covers from the lamps in our house. Among the other houses, still submissively dark, only our house was bright, the light shining through the pumpkin leaves and illuminating the big glossy fruit.[19]

Yamada Fūtarō feared that, with the emperor's words of surrender, the Allies—Americans, British, Chinese—would soon be landing in the tens of thousands or perhaps hundreds of thousands, and he foresaw the "terrifying moral, spiritual, economic and emotional anguish" into which this would plunge the Japanese. Then he took up the question, not addressed by other diarists, of the likely fate of the emperor:

What will happen to the emperor? Surely he will abdicate, but something more drastic may occur. According to the newspapers, at the final meeting in his presence the emperor said, "When We think of Our country being reduced to ashes, whatever may happen to Our person does not merit consideration." At this, they say, members of the cabinet all sobbed aloud. Someone said, "Having heard these words of His Majesty, even if the unthinkable should afflict His Majesty, we shall fulfill our duty to erect a shrine to his memory, however small, regardless of the wishes of the Allied forces."[20]

Yamada did not say so plainly, but no doubt he, like the cabinet members, thought it likely that the Americans would execute the emperor. He then considered how the Japanese should behave when the foreign troops of the Occupation arrived:

Now that our great undertaking [the war] has come to an end, we should in solemn silence, cleanly dressed, meet the enemy, maintaining an attitude so correct and so commanding as to make the proud enemy feel ashamed. Fireworks inspired by the present violent emotions can only increase and prolong the suffering of the ordinary people. We must do everything possible to shorten the enemy's occupation. One flaring up of impatience today may delay by several years the day of our revival.[21]

Yamada wrote harshly about those who were already joyfully proclaiming that a new Japan would be born from the ashes of the old, discredited Japan:

Some say the old Japan has expired, that the Japan of "wealth and military strength" [fukoku kyōhei] is no more, that we should wash away everything, forget as quickly as possible the past, and build a Japan with a new sense of justice and a new beauty. —To think in such terms is absolutely impermissible. . . .

I say that Japan must again become a nation of wealth and military strength. To this purpose, we must dissect the war to the marrow, and with hatred and pain investigate the causes of our miserable defeat and meditate on them.

There is no point in thinking about a wholly new Japan or the like. Even if one does, it's not something that can be realized, and even if built, such a Japan would be fragile and shatter at the first crisis.

As we investigate the bitter past, a path opens up. One sees first of all that the biggest cause of the defeat was science and the inadequacy of scientific education.[22]

Yamada hoped that by giving the young a scientific education, Japan could once again be a powerful nation, and the young people themselves would be unlike the emotional, easily swayed Japanese of the present: "We will create children with healthy bodies and cool-headed minds. In a word, these Japanese will be like steel. Their senses will be beautiful as steel, their bodies strong as steel, their minds fresh and firm as steel."

But that was only a dream. Yamada was dismayed to learn, so soon after the end of the war, that people had begun to show contempt for the military. A soldier who went, as was the practice during the war, to the head of the line at a railway station was told by the woman at the ticket window, "Soldiers go to the end of the line." Everyone who heard this story said in anger, "Why didn't the soldier slam that she-fox?"[23]

Others were already planning to cooperate with the Americans. A friend of Yamada's, the son of the owner of a major pharmaceutical company, told him on the night of August 15, "The intelligent thing to do now is shake hands with the Americans. My company plans to start immediately manufacturing cosmetics and to make money selling them to American women." When another friend said, "You can't do that," he answered with a laugh, "Anyone who thinks that way will certainly end up a beggar."[24]

Even after the emperor had publicly announced his acceptance of the terms of the Potsdam Declaration and the palace rebels had committed suicide or been subdued, elements of the military refused to admit that Japan had surrendered. On August 16, Osaragi Jirō heard that a plane had scattered leaflets saying, in the name of the commandant of the Navy Air Corps, that the emperor's rescript had been coerced by senior officials and that the Navy Air Corps would fight to the end.

Other planes dropped leaflets claiming that the Special Attack Force was still in existence and asserting that the atomic bombs were not as effective as people supposed.[25]

Rumors abounded, as usual. Osaragi heard that inhabitants of Tokyo were afraid that local Koreans, taking advantage of the termination of the war, would become violent and seize what food was available. A friend of Osaragi's had it from his doctor that the Americans would probably land at Kamakura the following day. Various high-ranking officers were reported to have committed suicide, but most of the rumors were untrue. A governmental directive was issued ordering women and children to flee the cities, and the train stations were soon filled with refugees. Rumor had it that many women had taken to the mountains and were hiding, determined to foil potential American rapists by killing themselves by swallowing the potassium cyanide capsules they carried with them.[26] Osaragi heard that police officers in Yokohama were deserting their posts and running away. Osaragi asked, "Because even officials act in this manner, the people naturally become confused and raise an outcry. What has happened to the beautiful and superior qualities of the Japanese?"[27] Three days later, Osaragi heard that many mothers in Zaimokuza were terrified because they had heard that American soldiers fed babies to their dogs.[28]

As early as August 16, the day after the war ended, diarists were reflecting on the roles they themselves had played during the war. Takami Jun wrote, "I was not one who wished for the defeat of Japan. I am not happy about the defeat. I wanted Japan to win somehow, and to this end exerted my meager strength in my own way. Now my heart is filled with great sorrow. It is filled with love of Japan and the Japanese."

But immediately afterward, he recalled an unpleasant incident. It had taken place in Harbin in November 1944. He had gone to a cabaret where a Russian orchestra played and Russian women danced. All the customers were Japanese officers, befuddled with vodka and singing at the top of their lungs. They behaved in such a disgraceful manner toward the Russian musicians and dancers that Takami felt deeply ashamed of his countrymen. Now the war had ended, and he wrote,

Although I did not write it in my diary, I recall wondering at the time what would happen if such Japanese won the war. This was not the only such occasion. There were things that brought back this uncertainty, again and again. I love Japan and the Japanese, and that is precisely why I cannot tolerate such Japanese. And I could not tolerate *Nippon shugi* opinions, which, by forgiving and indulging such Japanese, had the effect of steadily increasing their numbers.[29]

On August 21, less than a week after the emperor read his rescript, Takami described how profoundly he felt his dilemma as a Japanese writer:

I was relieved when I learned the war had ended. This meant the end of the tyranny of being told that love stories were not permitted, that three-cornered relationships must not be described, that adultery was a forbidden subject, and so on. I thought that the day when I could write freely would soon arrive. I was relieved, telling myself I could make a new start. But this "joy" was given me at an extremely high price, defeat in the war. I now feel astonished that I could have had such thoughts. I can only feel ashamed of the self that felt relieved. To exaggerate a bit, relief constituted a traitorous emotion. During the war, things were so terrible, what with the indiscriminate pressure against freedom of speech, the despotism of some Japanese (some of the military), and the sloppy ways of Japan and the Japanese, that I often thought that if we won the war it would be terrible—if we won the war with such things unchanged, Japan and the whole world would be in darkness. But now that I am confronted with the reality of defeat, I cannot but be ashamed of those feelings of mine. One simply cannot say calmly that Japan was doomed to lose the war because the country was full of such ugly defects and such self-conceit. At any rate, both Japan and I have have had the reality of defeat hammered into us. The misfortune of the defeat is mine. I wonder if I, too, should not have done something important for Japan's sake to prevent the present situation from befalling us. Instead of complaining in vain about the oppressive controls on freedom of speech, should I not have actively opposed and prevented corruption and degeneration? Should I not have striven, if only in a small way, to prevent the present misfortune from occurring?

It's inconceivable that we might have won. That's one point on which one can't overrate Japan. But there must surely have been some solution that would not have entailed a miserable defeat like today's. We should have worked harder to find it, but we did not, and I feel deeply ashamed.

I am now consumed with fiercely patriotic sentiments.[30]

THE ENTRY for August 16, 1945, in Yamada Fūtarō's diary is unusually long, reflecting the many confused thoughts that passed through the young man's mind after hearing the emperor's broadcast. He concluded,

I cannot but be overwhelmed by profound sadness. This is because my sole desire and aim at present is to wreak vengeance on the enemy. I can't think of anything else now, even if we must fight another, bitter war in order to bring about the rebirth of Japan. But I must suppress all sentimental, idealistic thoughts. I must let this resolve mature deep within me. If the enemy's policy toward Japan is severe, I will in fact welcome it. I fear nothing more than that the enemy may treat Japan with generosity, corrupting us peacefully.[1]

Yamada was determined to hate the Americans and feared any kindness that might weaken Japanese resolve to avenge the defeat. When, early in September, he briefly visited Kyoto, he wrote,

> Kyoto survives. It actually annoys me that Kyoto should have survived. It annoys me that the Americans spared Kyoto as a place for their own sightseeing. Most people, however, say they spared Kyoto and Nara as cultural monuments and not as "playgrounds" for themselves, but in the final analysis, that's what they will become. In other words, it shows what a surplus of strength they have, which is all the more annoying. The Soviet Union would probably have bombed Kyoto mercilessly. And if there were an old capital in America, Japan, of course, would not have had the slightest hesitation about demolishing it. This is true, at any rate, of the military.[2]

Yamada would maintain his anti-American stance even when, as occasionally happened, he could not help but recognize that a given feature of the American presence was beneficial. He seemed determined never to let down his guard because, as someone who had spent the war years at his studies, rather than on the battlefield, he believed that he had a special responsibility:

> Countless young men died. Most of those who survived were left with heads emptied by the war, and went bad. The fine minds of the few who kept studying all through the war, almost without break, must become the sole motivating force of the new Japan. We will engrave this heavy responsibility in our hearts and vow to Heaven that we will carry it through.[3]

Yamada noted that two officers had committed seppuku that day before the Imperial Palace and wondered how many other Japanese had chosen to die rather than become subjects of a foreign power.[4] There were not very many.

Unno Jūza, on hearing that America and Britain would probably accept a Japanese offer to surrender, decided that he could not live under foreign rule. On August 12, it seemed to him that "the day had come" for suicide. He consulted with his wife, who said, "It's better to die, if enemy soldiers are going to land here." Their children, after holding a conference of their own, told their parents, "We'll eat whatever food is left, then die." The older son said, "I want to kill an enemy soldier before I die." The second son, who had lately learned at school the slogan "Seven Lives for My Country," kept repeating it. Unno wrote the words on his front door. He said in his diary, "It would be easy for me to die by myself. But to take my beloved family with me—it won't be easy to kill myself after first disposing of them. One's feelings may well change in the act of killing. But perhaps it can be done simply, if one actually does it, and this may be a groundless fear."[5]

On August 13, after further discussion with his wife, they decided that the whole family would die. But two days later, after hearing the emperor's broadcast, they were so emotionally exhausted that Unno decided to postpone their deaths to the following night, after a last family gathering. Unno spent August 16 reading *Taigi* (*The Supreme Duty*), the posthumous work of the war hero Lieutenant Colonel Sugimoto Gorō (1900–1937), a text that combines Zen Buddhism and emperor-worship. The conviction gradually permeated Unno that the Way of a Japanese was to become one with the emperor, to eliminate the ego, and to discard mind and body, serving the emperor.

That night, his wife could not sleep. In the middle of the night she got up. Unno, guessing that she intended to kill herself, admonished her: " 'You must give up the thought of dying.' It was painful to admonish her. It was like telling her to accept pain and humiliation worse than death. My wife wept. Then I lost my courage. I couldn't look her in the face, but there was nothing I could do. In the end, she yielded. I had decided to follow *Taigi*."[6]

The last entry in Unno's diary is for December 31:

Ah, the 20th year of Shōwa [1945]! It was a dreadful year, unspeakable. I found life in death, and in life I was pursued by death, back and forth, again and again, between the two, sometimes becoming a living corpse, sometimes weeping a man's tears over heartbreaking sorrow. And the reality of the defeat has not revealed itself completely. It will extend into the years to come. The difficulty of living!

However, my path is settled. I shall devote my last energy, as long as life is left me, to the spread of scientific techniques and to the promotion of science fiction.[7]

Few well-known civilians committed suicide, no matter how devoted to the imperial cause. By contrast, Takami Jun quoted a report that during the first four days after the announcement of the agreement reached at Potsdam on the future of Germany, 1200 people in Berlin, 600 in Leipzig, 450 in Hamburg, and 300 in Cologne had committed suicide. He said he felt ashamed before Germany.[8]

The best-known postwar suicide was a failure, General Tōjō Hideki's botched attempt on September 11, after hearing that the Americans had issued a warrant for his arrest. Yamada Fūtarō wrote with scorn, "The first reaction of every Japanese, on learning that General Tōjō had shot himself, was to cry out, 'So he's done it at last!' They probably breathed a sigh of relief along with shock and sadness on learning that what was bound to come had in fact come." But later on, learning the details, they were not so favorable. Yamada wrote,

Why didn't General Tōjō kill himself the night of the broadcast, like a man, the way Army Minister Anami [Korechika] did? Why didn't General Tōjō use a Japanese sword like Army Minister Anami? It was obvious that an arrest warrant would be issued, but he went on living, reluctant to die. Then, like a foreigner, he used a pistol. He aimed at himself and missed. A Japanese can't help but give a bitter smile.[9]

Takami's reactions to Tōjō's failed suicide were similar:

If he had something to look forward to, something that had kept him from committing suicide up to this point, why didn't he bear the unbearable and allow himself to be taken by the police? Why was it not until now that, in a state of excitement, he chose suicide? If death was what he wanted, he should have killed himself on the day of the Imperial Rescript. If he wanted to stay alive, he should have stood in a court of law and reiterated his beliefs.

There could be no greater disgrace. And, on top of that, in his overwrought state he failed to kill himself, adding disgrace to disgrace.[10]

Despite his anger about the ending of the war, Yamada did not abandon his rational outlook. When he heard on August 17 that extremists had set fires in the houses of two former prime ministers, Suzuki Kantarō and Hiranuma Kiichirō, he commented, "What stupidity! If they can't bear the humiliation of the defeat, they should quietly slit their bellies. This is no time to display in Japan the foolishness of washing blood with blood."[11]

"Patriots" ripped from the walls notices announcing the surrender. Still others pasted posters of their own at railway stations in Tokyo, denouncing the surrender and threatening to shoot and kill anyone who defaced their posters. The Fujisawa Air Unit of the Yokosuka Naval Station, flatly refusing to accept the surrender, scattered leaflets from the sky saying that even though the parents had surrendered, the children had not.[12]

During the two weeks following the emperor's broadcast, innumerable rumors kept the Japanese, desperately eager to know their fate, in a state of anxious uncertainty. One story had it that the Japanese army in the Philippines had started a general offensive, but most rumors were disheartening. Yamada heard that American troops had landed at Shimizu and that Chinese soldiers who had landed at Nagoya had begun to requisition food. He also heard on August 17 that there were 40,000 American soldiers in Tokyo.[13] The next day, he heard a rumor that 300,000 Americans had gone ashore at Yokohama.[14] With the passage of time, most rumors faded away, but some continued to make the rounds until they were forgotten or totally discredited.

Takami was deeply moved by a brief article in a newspaper saying that foreign detainees had offered their rations to war victims. He felt ashamed. Again and again, Takami would speak of shame, either his own or Japan's. He contrasted the generosity of the foreigners with the heartlessness of members of the military and government officials who, according to rumors, were looting emergency stores of food:

> I have yet to hear one story to the effect that the military have given even a portion of the loot to unfortunate war victims. As a Japanese, it is shaming. . . . Wherever one goes, one hears stories of officers who have taken home massive amounts of military supplies. There is also a rumor that the landing force may investigate such incidents as acts of larceny. If this should happen, it would be a disgrace, the shame of Japan.[15]

After years of glorification of the military, disillusion set in with great rapidity. The newspapers were still trying to determine the causes of Japan's defeat, but hatred of the war (regardless of why Japan was defeated) began to be expressed. Takami wrote on August 21 that an article in the *Mainichi shinbun* was the first to make public the people's growing opposition to the military. People had come to believe that the military were indifferent to the suffering of victims of the bombings.[16]

On September 1, Yamada Fūtarō wrote,

> The newspapers are slowly beginning to attack the militarists [*gunbatsu*]. They speak of "out-and-out ringleaders of the black market," of how "with their power they practiced despotism and with their swords choked discussion," and how "with His Majesty as their shield, they demanded belief in the supralogical [*kamigakari shinnen*]." And the newspapers blithely say, "We, members of the press, are ashamed that we submitted blindly to this coercion." The past ten years have been an unprecedented period of shame in the history of the Japanese press.[17]

Reflecting on his own experiences, Yamada related his struggle to accept, against his own intelligence, the ideology of the military and how, despite his distrust of irrationality, he had persuaded himself it was necessary to winning the war:

> On a number of occasions, I felt doubts about the illogical, irrational beliefs, and perhaps at times I thought of the eloquent fanatics surrounding me as idiotic or incomprehensible. To this day, I am comparatively less affected by fanaticism than other people.
>
> Yet, to tell the truth, I continued to fear these beliefs shared by everybody else. I felt the helplessness of one who sees truth, though but faintly, even in the midst of the turbid waters of fanaticism. It was not apprehension. It was because I continued to think, in the midst of the madness of war, that being possessed by such illogical assertions as "Japan, the Land of the Gods, can never be defeated" or "Spiritual strength is stronger than science" might be necessary as motivating forces for victory. It was because of the frightening suspicion that my logical manner of thinking might be mistaken in the present human world, a world that better be described as animal.
>
> But the illogical proved to be illogical, and the irrational was irrational to the end.
>
> I suppose that the new tone in the newspapers will soon completely change the Japanese view of the war and their view of the world. The more fervently a man embraced supralogical thought up to now, the more he will be engulfed in the new wave, and he will lose himself in it because it stems from emotionally the same temperament. —The same human being who thought of enemy soldiers as demons and who ran about frantically killing them, before a year has passed will look on himself as a world criminal and begin to feel blind faith in "peace" or "culture."[18]

Yamada was correct in predicting that many Japanese in a remarkably short period of time would display a complete reversal of behavior.

Less than two weeks had passed since the war ended, but an outcry of indignation was raised when it was discovered that although victims of the bombing were about to spend the winter virtually naked, the erstwhile heroes of the army were busy stealing government property. The only excuse for their thievery was that if they did not swipe the army goods, the Americans might confiscate them.[19] Yamada commented that during the war Japan may have been intolerant, but at least it was honest. Since the war, Japan had lost even this last virtue.[20]

The signing on the battleship *Missouri* of the instrument of surrender excited a comment from Yamada: "Japan from this day has lost its status as an independent nation." He heard that the flag at the mast of the *Missouri* was the same one that had fluttered over Commodore Matthew Perry's "black ships" when, almost a hundred years earlier, he had come to open Japan. He also heard that General Arthur Percival was being flown to the Philippines in order to be present at the signing of the treaty of surrender with General Yamashita Tomoyuki, the victor at Singapore in 1941. Yamada sarcastically commented, "Love for the theatrical is surely a basic human instinct."[21]

Even before the first American troops landed, there was a new atmosphere in Japan. No order came from the government ending the censorship of the press, but writers intuitively realized that the defeat had liberated them from the hated restrictions. On August 17, Takami Jun felt emboldened to write, "I would not say now that my work up to the present has been a total lie, but I can say that under the restrictions, which grew worse by the day, I wrote nothing that was not a product of self-deception, a soothing of my conscience, a forcing of myself to go forward in a direction not in my heart, an endurance with clenched teeth."[22]

On August 20, Prince Higashikuni Naruhiko (1887–1990), the newly appointed prime minister, made a radio broadcast to the nation, repeated several times, in which he declared that the government had a plan for saving the *kokutai*.[23] Everyone listened with bated breath, wondering if his next words would be something on the order of "If the enemy attempts to destroy the *kokutai*, we will resume the war, and ask every last one of you to rise up." However, as Yamada stated, the prince's voice was one of extreme despair and grief; there were no threats of resuming the war.[24]

On the same day, Takami, during a conversation with the *Mainichi* reporter Sawahiraki Susumu, said he thought that the newspapers should apologize for the misinformation they had printed: "I fully understand that the newspapers could print nothing but lies. The people understand it too. But, all the same, for the newspapers not to feel any compunctions— It's not only the newspapers. It's a question that affects every commentator and intellectual. We writers must equally apologize." Sawahiraki answered, "I wonder if there is any feeling at the newspapers today that they owe the public an apology. They seem to be very happy that from now on they will be able to publish a free newspaper. It's shocking."[25] Takami wrote that he was happy to have met a reporter, though he might be the only one, who thought along these lines.

The top article in the *Yomiuri shinbun* the next day predicted that literature, which had long been tormented, would now gain its freedom.[26] Takami was aware of the optimism infusing the article, but it did not cheer him, knowing how unlikely it was that the newspaper would apologize for its wartime pusillanimity. Later that day, he wrote in greater detail his reactions to the article:

This morning I was writing in a hurry and could not clearly express what was in my heart. I wrote merely "it did not cheer me," but my feelings were actually far more intense and unpleasant. I was furious.

How could they have the effrontery to say such things? That's what made me furious. I don't think the point of the article is mistaken. It's quite correct. I agree. But it makes my blood boil to hear them say things that are undoubtedly true, but without sadness, without self-examination, without expression, without consistency. They always glibly come out with whatever suits the particular occasion. I can't stand their mechanical, inhuman nature. A bare month ago, they were bellowing that art and science existed for the sake of the war, that the war was the sole guiding principle—and now, the same newspapers wipe their mouths and, as if nothing has happened, have the impudence to exalt the great importance of the arts and sciences. Their shameless pose as "leaders" makes me sick. I would like to tell them to stop treating us as half-wits. Now that we've lost the war, are they protecting the arts? No thanks for that kind of protection. And I don't want your uncalled-for meddling. After all your interference and oppression, what are you up to now? It was because of the inhuman interference and oppression, the mistaken controls and guidance, that we lost the war. Shutting your eyes to self-examination, you once again, with effrontery and shamelessness, assume the role of our leaders. Enough is enough.[27]

On August 22, Takami attended a meeting of the board of directors of the Bunpō. The sole subject of discussion was whether the organization should continue. The secretariat favored dissolution. Togawa Sadao, an extreme nationalist, might have been expected to advocate continuation, but he quite correctly said that the society had been founded to aid the prosecution of the Greater East Asia War, and now that this objective had ceased to exist, he also favored dissolution. Opposition to the decision was voiced, however, by one member whose name Takami rendered as "XX," apparently still hesitant to write it openly.

The man produced a leaflet from his briefcase that, he said, he was distributing to servicemen. A certain air squadron had vowed to fight to the end, and the members had resolved, if their fight was unsuccessful, to slit their abdomens and die. "I have asked their permission to join them," the man said, his eyes shining with a strange glitter. He declared that acceptance of the Potsdam Declaration had been a Jewish plot and cursed the new cabinet as being under the control of the Sumitomo *zaibatsu* (conglomerate). Takami disagreed with every word the man said, but kept silent. He sardonically wished that even one literary man of *Nippon shugi* convictions had committed a really splendid seppuku.[28]

Ozaki Shirō, a permanent director of the Bunpō, arrived late at the meeting. He had long been an advocate of *Nippon shugi* and, on the recommendation of the Cabinet Information Bureau, he had been appointed a permanent director of the association. Takami relates,

I had supposed that either the defeat would make him fiercely fanatical or else heartbreaking emotions would rend him utterly desolate. In fact, he was extremely cheerful. When asked what he planned to do, he criticized the opinion of Kikuchi Kan, who, when expressing his views on the radio the other day, said something to the effect that writers should give their all for literature. Ozaki said that the task of the writer was not to expatiate on the literature of the future but to size up the present realities and to face them squarely and realistically. I felt he was putting up a shrewd front. He himself feels not the slightest responsibility for the present situation, but blames other people—the military or whoever—for having done wrong. It was enough to make me tremble with rage.

He speaks of the "present realities," but does he suppose he bears no responsibility for creating them? It's not so much that he adroitly jumped onto the bandwagon and cooperated in the brutal suppression of freedom of speech; did he not actively play a leading role? Was he not a convinced practitioner of the strategy of keeping the masses culturally ignorant? Now he comes out with the charge that the military were mistaken, but at the time, was it not he who, protected by the military, used the borrowed authority of the tiger to perform the tricks of the fox?

If I may use myself as an example, I could not bear to see literature rapidly sinking into nonliterature, and I went so far as to write a piece on the powerlessness of literature, saying that literature has its own role and that it was misguided to attempt to make it play the same role as bullets. I wrote in a very conciliatory manner. And what did he reply?

"If the attitude of maintaining the purity of literature within the traditions of the literary world still survives, we must be aware that not only is this mere self-complacency but, combined with the distorted character of journalism, connects it with the enemy character of liberalism."

He called me a traitor. He denounced me. Now this "traitor" weeps for the misfortune of his country. I weep because I, too, bear responsibility. And the *Nippon shugi* advocate Ozaki Shirō, who labeled me a traitor, today calmly urges that we look directly at present realities and confront them. He who formerly cursed "enemy liberalists" now talks like one.

He also had this to say . . . "It would be truly lamentable if a man of letters, resolved to preserve his purity in journalism, decided that the way to do this was by going contrary to the destiny of his country."

When the country was defeated, he blithely made up his mind to go "contrary to the destiny of his country." What a lamentable thing it is! People like him pushed Japan down into the "present realities" of today. And people like myself who tolerated such actions are not without blame![29]

On August 29, Takami wrote, "Freedom of speech, publication, assembly and association seem gradually to becoming a reality. It cheers my heart, Now that I think of it, we were in the middle ages. It was a dark-age government, a government of fear—However, I don't suppose that true freedom can be granted. Unless Japan becomes more grown-up . . ." Takami did not finish his thought, but although the Americans had not yet landed and still exerted no direct influence on Japanese internal affairs, the Japanese already felt that the basic freedoms were within their grasp. Japanese cynics would soon remark that the United States had given Japan a ration of freedom, but they tend to ignore this spontaneous development. I am tempted to suggest that the process of democratization might have taken place even without the assistance of the Americans.

On August 30, the newspapers reported in detail an interview given to the press two days earlier by the prime minister, Prince Higashikuni Naruhiko. When asked why Japan had lost the war, the prince attributed the defeat to three causes: the acute depletion of fighting strength, the atomic bombs, and the entry of the Soviet Union into the war. He also mentioned the steady growth of defeatism among the military and officials, and the lowering of the people's morality. The prince urged the Japanese, when rebuilding the country, to ponder the spirit of the Oath in Five Articles of Emperor Meiji as a guide to reconstruction[30] and promised to present to the next session of the Diet figures on the losses Japan had sustained, hiding nothing. Declaring that the Japanese people had long been gagged, he stated that henceforth there would be freedom of speech and assembly. He deplored the existence of government-sponsored political parties that had kept other views from being heard and had refused to allow freedom of the press. He hoped that from now on, the people would express their opinions vigorously.

After a long and terrible war had barely ended, the highest official in the government (who had been a major general) was openly voicing sentiments that had been strictly forbidden two weeks earlier. Takami was dazzled by Prince Higashikuni's frankness: "This is what we have longed for, but have never been given. It did my heart good. The feeling was truly optimistic. Why were we never given this kind of government before the defeat? To think that such optimism could be given only as sad compensation for the defeat!"[31]

The results of the new policies were immediate. Osaragi Jirō noted that American radio broadcasts from Saipan were no longer being jammed. The newspapers had taken on an American-style openness, and the number of dispatches from abroad had increased.[32]

Less attractive aspects of the new regime began to appear at the same time. Takami pasted into his diary an advertisement that had appeared in the *Tōkyō shinbun*, placed by the "Association for Special Comfort Facilities," calling for job applicants. Takami guessed that the purpose of the association was to provide women for the "comfort" of the army of occupation. He expected that soon there would be Japanese men and women on the Tokyo streets calling "Hey!" or "Come on!" to passing American soldiers.[33] On August 30, he reported that bars, cafés, and cabarets had been opened as "comfort facilities" in Yokohama.[34] Osaragi noted on the same day that an order had been issued prohibiting restaurants and geisha houses in Yokosuka from closing, no doubt in consideration for the needs of the American fleet.

Takami was resigned to the American presence, but each sign in English, put up for the benefit of arriving Americans, irritated him and brought forth ironic comments. He noticed that pieces of white paper

had been pasted onto subway billboards and guessed that they concealed such slogans as "Annihilate the Arrogant Enemy!" and "Certain
Victory!" On September 8, he noticed in the Shinbashi Station a sign in
English: "Way Out." He wondered, "When was it that roman-letter station signs were all blotted out? Roman-letter signs have appeared again.
I hear the Tokyo authorities hope government buildings, banks, and
major places of business will put up signs in English indicating what
they are."[35]

On the same day, Takami saw his first American soldier. The man
looked "like a cheerful, mischievous kid."[36] This was only a momentary
impression, but Takami was characterizing a major difference between
the American Occupation of Japan and the Japanese occupation of
China. There would soon be stories of American servicemen behaving
riotously, stealing watches, illegally entering people's houses, and
worse.[37] But on September 14, Takami wrote,

> There was an American soldier on the jam-packed train. He was
> talking with a Japanese. It seemed quite natural, as if he had been
> in Japan for a long time. There was something very city-like about
> him. He gave one the feeling of being democratic.
>
> I mentally sketched a Japanese soldier who has just arrived in
> China. When he sees a Chinese, he says, "*Oi, nii kō.*" He makes no
> distinction between a coolie and a university student. The soldier,
> originally a peasant, when he arrests a Chinese gentleman says,
> "*Oi, atchi e ike.*" He treats a Chinese like a dog or a pig.[38]

On September 21, Takami wrote,

> The streets of Tokyo swarm with American servicemen. One
> sees them wherever one goes. But no matter where I have gone, I
> have never seen an American soldier strike a Japanese or behave
> with an air of superiority or in a menacing manner.
>
> In China, wherever I went, I invariably saw Japanese soldiers
> lording it over the Chinese. Wherever I went, I invariably saw
> scenes of Japanese hitting Chinese.

The Americans respect the Japanese as human beings, probably because they themselves are respected as human beings. The Japanese maltreated other races because they themselves had been maltreated by other Japanese. This occurred because the rights and freedom of the individual were completely denied. In Japan there was no respect for human beings.[39]

He moved on to the hitherto forbidden question of the emperor. In the closing stages of the war, he had told his wife that he was ready to die for the emperor. But learning on September 28 that the emperor had visited General Douglas MacArthur, he wrote,

I was astonished to read in the newspaper that the emperor had called on General MacArthur. Perhaps it was nothing to be surprised at, considering this is a defeated country.

Nothing like His Majesty the Emperor personally going to a foreigner's residence had happened before. It has certainly come as a great shock to the Japanese. Perhaps in another couple of dozen years it will not seem so strange, but now, yes, it gives a really strange feeling. We have been taught that His Majesty the Emperor is a sacred being whom we cannot approach. . . .

I believe that the ideal that Japan held up, "Asia for the Asiatics," will unquestionably flare up again, whenever it may be. This does not mean that I expect a conflict between East and West, nor do I hope for a battle between the white and yellow races. I pray for a liberation of the East groaning under the yoke of the West. I hope to see the day when men of the East and West live together under the name of common humanity without one being dominated by the other.[40]

On September 29, the well-known photograph of Emperor Hirohito and General MacArthur standing side by side was printed in the newspapers. It was unprecedented. Takami mused that perhaps people in the future would think of it as something quite normal, but at present it went against all the assumptions of the Japanese. On the following day, the newspapers that had published the photograph were banned by the Japanese authorities. MacArthur's headquarters responded by canceling the ban and ordering new measures be taken to guarantee freedom of the press and of speech. Takami was ecstatic: "Now one can write anything at all, freely! We can publish anything at all, freely! This is the first freedom I have known since I was born."[41]

> When I think back to the fact that freedom, which naturally should have been given by the people's own government, could not be given, and instead has been bestowed for the first time by the military forces of a foreign country occupying their own, I cannot escape feelings of shame. I am ashamed as someone who loves Japan, ashamed for Japan's sake.
>
> It would be understandable if an occupation army, coming in after a war in which we were defeated, had restricted our freedom, but the opposite has occurred—freedom has been guaranteed. What a shaming thing! Our own country's government robbed the people of almost every freedom, and we did nothing to remedy this loss until a notification arrived from the Army of Occupation. What a humiliation![42]

The precious gift of liberty from a very recent enemy brought Takami both joy and, above all, shame. As the Occupation wore on, he experienced much less of either emotion, but Takami had resumed his career as a writer.

THE SURRENDER of Japan and the end of the war brought liberation to some writers, especially those who had suffered because of their left-wing convictions. But most, irrespective of their political beliefs, were downcast by the defeat of their country and apprehensive about what the future might bring. The abolition of censorship was, of course, welcomed by everyone, though it would soon be discovered, to the writers' dismay, that the Americans, despite their proclaimed ideal of freedom of speech, would censor publications and even private letters.[1] This highly irritating censorship did not, however, prevent the postwar years from being one of the major periods of Japanese literature.

The death of the novelist Shimaki Kensaku (1903–1945) on August 17, the first literary event of the postwar era, came as a shock to writers. Many civilians but not one important writer had died during the war; Shimaki might be considered the first wartime victim, though his illness was not directly related to the war.[2] Takami Jun, perhaps more than anyone else, was affected by Shimaki's death. Both men had been involved with Marxist activities in the 1930s and, after being arrested, had sworn to the police that they had renounced their left-wing beliefs. This repudiation had been especially painful for Shimaki, an intensely serious man who, unlike Takami, found no solace in drink or the pleasures of Asakusa. Takami wrote, "People say that Shimaki and his writings are boring, that his novels aren't novels, that he isn't a novelist. It's the sort of thing I might have said, but although I am Shimaki's exact opposite as a human being and in the way I live, I never said such things."[3] A bond of parallel, painful experiences kept Takami from joining others in their mockery of the intensely serious Shimaki.

Shimaki's first novel, *Saiken* (*Reconstruction*), published in 1937, was banned by the government because it portrayed with sympathy a man imprisoned for left-wing convictions. Shimaki intended to write a second part to the novel, in which the man would reject Marxism, but he never got the chance. The shock of having the book banned, and the loss of much-needed income, was immense, and it would not have been surprising if Shimaki had killed himself. Instead, he produced the long novel *Seikatsu no tankyū* (*Quest for Life*, 1937). This work does not denounce left-wing thought, nor does it, in the manner of *Nippon shugi* writers, proclaim the supremacy of Japan, but it was nevertheless enthusiastically received by the authorities because it conveyed to readers the kind of productive life that was possible in a time of national emergency.

Shimaki traveled to Manchukuo in 1939 to observe the results of Japanese colonization. On the whole, he was sympathetic to the colonists, most of whom had settled in China to escape extreme poverty in Japan. Shimaki did not question the legitimacy of the Japanese occupation of Chinese territory, but he criticized other, less fundamental policies. Japanese authorities normally were loath to accept criticism of any kind, but they accepted Shimaki's: his criticism was aimed at improving conditions for the colonists, and he did not urge ending the occupation of Manchukuo.

Later works strengthened the impression that Shimaki had truly given up leftist thought, but when Takami visited the hospital room where Shimaki lay dying, Shimaki's wife told him that Shimaki, on hearing that the war had ended, had said he intended to make a fresh start.[4] Takami commented, "Shimaki died without being able to make his fresh start. At the thought, I feel worse than if I had been split in two." The "fresh start" may have been a second change of affiliation, this time a return to his earlier political beliefs.

After the funeral, Shimaki's friends, gathered to remember him, discussed the present-day situation in Japan. Several spoke out against the militarists who still resisted the imperial rescript that ended the war. By now, such condemnation was neither dangerous nor even unusual. Others favored resisting the Americans when they landed. In his diary account of the discussion, Takami gave his own opinion:

> Resistance would be fine if there were any chance that it might win the war for us, but it is obvious that there is no possibility of victory, that we have lost the war. If, knowing that they are doomed to fail, they persist in their rashness, they may well lose their last line of defense, the *kokutai*. No, we'll be made into a colony. Can't the resisters realize this? The ones who got Japan into this miserable predicament are the arrogant militarists who even now are still crying for resistance. The militarists have made a mess of Japan, and they're still tormenting the people. Is their ultimate goal the destruction of Japan? They know that, in any case, they will be punished as war criminals. Is what they're doing now an act of desperation, intended to drag the whole people down with them?[5]

Takami kept silent during the discussion, but he wrote in his diary, "Open criticism of the military clique is certainly a big change. To record such changes, moment by moment, is the task of the diarist.

Once a change has taken place, nobody can recall when and how it happened."[6]

Takami's diary carefully records many changes in Tokyo and Kamakura during the immediate postwar days. Even on days when little occurred that required him to take notice, Takami never lost sight of the duty of the diarist to set down everything that people of the future might want to know about the era.

Nagai Kafū's diary is much less concerned with future readers than with the privations he suffered. After the war ended, he remained for a week or two in Okayama, but there was nothing to occupy him and the rations were extremely skimpy. He returned to Tokyo and went directly to the house of his cousin Kineya Gosō, only to be informed that he had left for Atami a month earlier. Kafū followed Gosō to Atami.

Kafū's life in Atami was not enjoyable. He characterized Atami: "It's the kind of place where businessmen and vulgar tourists are expected to squander their money. Its one redeeming feature is that it does not smell of the military."[7] He sometimes spent the whole day in bed reading, hoping that books would help him forget the pangs of hunger. He told himself that he should write something before the weather got too cold, but his stomach was so empty that he lacked the energy to write.[8]

On September 9, he received a letter from a friend in Tokyo describing how clusters of American soldiers now sauntered through the Tokyo streets. The letter added, "The disbanding of the wartime bureaucracy has truly swept away the dark clouds of many years' standing. It is like looking up at a clear autumn sky. This is the great, wonderful event of recent times."[9]

Kafū agreed. He had always hated the military, which made him tolerant of the American presence. The next day, a neighbor related to Kafū that, after boarding the last train back to Atami from Tokyo, he had been forced to give up his seat when some forty or fifty American soldiers came aboard. Kafū, instead of expressing annoyance at the overbearing Americans, wrote, "That's exactly how the Japanese used to treat the people of Manchuria. It's a case of crime and punishment."

Kafū, however, was far from cheerful. There was not enough rice to make gruel, even if it was mixed with beans or corn, and it was by no means easy to buy staples from the farmers. He heard predictions that starvation was on the way for the entire Japanese people, but he was even more depressed to hear men who only yesterday sang the praises of militarism now preach freedom and people's rights. He wrote, "Not one aspect of society one hears about or sees since the defeat but is the seed of heartbreak."

Friends in Tokyo expressed optimism, however, about the future of contemporary literature. Others expected a flourishing of the theater. And some wrote, "From now on, we must help one another to do work that, being optimistic, will be highly meaningful." Kafū dismissed such views as "platitudinous sentiments, no more than the language of advertisements. There is not a particle of truth in them." Only occasionally is his diary enlivened by a flash of humor, as when he described the emperor's visit to General MacArthur: "Yesterday morning His Majesty, dressed in mufti and traveling incognito, deigned to pay a visit on General of the Army Mr. Ma at the headquarters of the American Army in Akasaka."[10]

Kafū was slow to return to writing, but on October 2 he wrote the preface to a new book to be called *Raihōsha* (*The Visitor*), consisting of poems and short essays he had sent to friends during the war by way of thanks for gifts of food. The preface briefly described his wartime experiences and his joy on hearing that the war had ended.

On October 8, he began to assemble manuscripts for a proposed set of his complete works, possibly in twelve volumes. On October 15, Aoyama Toranosuke, the publisher of the forthcoming magazine *Shinsei* (*Vita Nuova*), visited Kafū. He asked for a manuscript and mentioned that the fee would be between ¥100 and ¥200 a *mai*.[11] Kafū commented, "Like the price of mackerel and horse mackerel, manuscript fees have been inflated. They astonish poor writers! It's amusing."[12]

Shinsei was an important new magazine. The inaugural issue, dated November 1, 1945, contains mainly political articles discussing the advent of the new era, but there are also literary essays.[13] The physical appearance of the magazine (which continued publication for twenty-three issues, until October 1948) could hardly have attracted readers. Each page, printed on coarse paper, has quadruple columns of minuscule type, and the few illustrations are crude. But *Shinsei* was popular in the immediate postwar period because it provided both intellectual stimulus for readers and a forum for writers (especially those who were already well known) where they could publish fiction and their impressions of the new Japan.

The first issue contains an essay by Aono Suekichi, "Sensō zakkan" (Impressions of the War), in which he recalled his mingled thoughts and emotions during the three and a half years when leaders "armed to the fingernails" completely controlled the country. For him, the war years were a great, empty hollow in his life, made bearable only by reading the poetry of Saigyō, Bashō, and Ryōkan.

Aono recalled an experience of two months earlier. He had been traveling on a night train. In his carriage was a boy, evidently a war victim, with some kind of malignant skin disease. The other passengers were brutally unfriendly to the boy and seemed ready to throw him from the train, when a man's voice emerged from the dark. He said, "I'm a soldier. I'm back from Java. The boy's pitiful. Wouldn't it be better for all of you to help him? I thought the Japanese were more beautiful, but is this what they are really like?"[14]

The soldier's words echoed in Aono's ears as the masks were torn from the faces of wartime leaders. He, too, had thought the Japanese were more beautiful. It was obvious that the Japanese have ability—otherwise, how to explain the great periods of Japanese culture?—but this aspect of the Japanese made him recall the soldier's question: "Is this what they are really like?" He wrote, "The Americans, in the interests of peace, as the victors, are sifting out the war criminals; should we not root out the criminals responsible for the degeneration of the Japanese? . . . Is this not the way for a new Japan of peace and culture to start? In that case, there is definitely a need for a general confession [*sōzange*] of the people."

Aono's call for a "general confession" was often repeated, and his call for a rooting out of those responsible for the spiritual defeat echoed views expressed by Ishikawa Tatsuzō (1905–1985) in his article "Nihon no saiken no tame ni" (For a Reconstruction of Japan), published in the October 1 issue of the *Mainichi shinbun*. Ishikawa not only wished to see those guilty of embroiling the Japanese in the war be punished, but urged a complete change in outlook of the Japanese people. He declared,

> Japan is a country of the past. That is my belief. I believe I have no choice but to think in these terms. Let us discard history, let us discard tradition, let us discard everything about which we could feel proud! . . . History is valuable. Tradition is valuable. But it was because we were so proud of their great value that we brought ruin to the empire.

Ishikawa looked forward to Japan becoming a democratic nation, but reminded readers that the peoples of the West had won democracy only after a struggle with their governments. The Japanese were as yet far from such self-awareness. They might establish the forms of democracy, but he hoped that the Occupation Army would remain in Japan until the reality of democracy had also been achieved.[15]

Japanese writers did not necessarily share Ishikawa's hope that the Americans would continue to guide Japan, but by December 1945 a great many Japanese were expressing admiration for democracy and the other virtues of the conquerors. Nagai Kafū's first contribution to *Shinsei*, "Amerika no omoide" (Memories of America), which appeared in the second issue, was, however, by no means adulatory. After admitting that his knowledge of the United States was dated (his stay in America was forty years earlier) and unlikely to be of relevance, Kafū wrote,

> If one went to America, supposing it was the country of freedom and democracy, quite a few things were likely to arouse one's indignation. The tendency was for social policy to be determined by public opinion, but because women participated in this opinion, quite a few of the effects were so stupid and superficial as to be intolerable to us. An example is *Salomé*, the opera by Richard Strauss. When it was about to be staged, performances were forbidden because of American-style public opinion.[16] Lafcadio Hearn was compelled by American-style public opinion to

sacrifice his love for a black woman. Gorky fled his country and went to New York, but could not remain in America long because of public opinion.[17]

These views, probably inspired by Kafū's annoyance with other people's overly enthusiastic admiration for the United States, also reflect his Francophilia. One of the few things in America he singled out for praise were the free libraries in New York, from which he had borrowed French books from the excellent collections.

Kafū published in the third issue of *Shinsei* his much-admired story "Kunshō" (The Decoration),[18] and in the March 1946 issue published four selections from his diary for 1945, followed by his diary for 1941. Kafū may not have intended originally to publish his wartime diaries,[19] but it was certainly easier than composing new stories and brought him welcome income. He made many small alterations in the texts of the diaries, but they remained essentially unchanged from the first versions.[20]

Kafū was by no means the only writer to publish his wartime diary. Uchida Hyakken, though after the war he refused almost all requests for articles, polished his diary for publication.[21] Kafū's postwar diary is in no sense a confession. It is largely concerned with the irritations of daily life and his worries about his finances. The entry for January 1, 1946, mentions that no dividends were paid on shares of stock and that there were rumors that a 20 percent tax would be levied on personal incomes:

Up to now I have enjoyed a steady income from stock dividends, but from this year on I will have to attempt to sustain myself by doing hackwork. I haven't been entirely without income since last autumn, but that was because some manuscripts I wrote out of boredom during the war happily did not get burned and I was able to sell them. Now, when I am close to seventy, I wonder if I shall be able to write as I did when I edited the periodical *Bunmei*.[22] My greatest misfortune was not to have died when I was about sixty. I shudder when I think of the future. Old and worn out, I may die of starvation. In order to save on breakfast, I read books in bed and wait until close to noon before I go to the kitchen downstairs and cook some onions and carrots to go with wheat gruel.[23]

Again and again, Kafū fulminated against such annoyances as a neighbor's noisy radio. Only when he reported rumors does the diary rise above complaints. On April 6, he recounted that when the Osaka police tried to arrest some Korean black-market operators, they resisted with weapons and were joined by Japanese colleagues. Along came some American MPs, who used their machine guns to mow down everyone in sight. This confrontation, Kafū stated, was not reported in the press because of censorship. His comment was that though the Americans preach freedom, they hide whatever is to their disadvantage.[24]

Kafū also maintained his interest in his old haunts, the houses of unlicensed prostitution in Tamanoi. In January 1946, there were only thirty houses, but soon there were more than a hundred. They charged foreign customers ¥130 to ¥140, but Japanese men paid only ¥100.[25]

On December 31, 1947, he wrote, "This has really been a bad year. In June, half my collection of books was stolen, and at the end of the year I was faced with nonpayment of royalties. But the greatest misfortune is that my withered old body lingers on, unable to die."[26]

Takami Jun had mixed feelings about the Occupation—gratitude for the freedom it had brought, anger over the discrepancy between the professed principles of the Americans and reality. But however involved he might become in interior debates about the Occupation, he never questioned the blessing of peace. On September 14, 1945, he attended the festival at the Tsuruoka Hachiman Shrine in Kamakura: "I went up to the altar to worship. *Kagura* dances were being performed. Girls were sitting all along the stone steps, quietly watching the *kagura*. Peace has truly come. The Japanese are truly a simple, peace-loving people."[27]

But such a mood did not last long. Two days later, he read in the newspaper a report released by the Supreme Commander of the Allied Powers on acts of atrocity performed by Japanese soldiers in the Philippines. They were horrifying, but Takami added, "If one is going to talk about atrocities, burning alive great numbers of civilians with incendiary bombs was unspeakably atrocious. The atrociousness of the atomic bombs needs no explanation. Atrocities by the victors are not discussed. Only the atrocities of the losers are condemned."[28]

On September 19, Takami reported in his diary that publication of the *Asahi shinbun* was halted for two days by command of MacArthur's headquarters. He commented wryly, "The *Asahi*, which during the war was looked at askance as being liberal and democratic, is now being punished for being patriotic."[29] But the same day also brought good news: "Vegetables and fish can now be sold freely. One can listen freely to broadcasts from foreign countries. Women may be given the vote. This is heartwarming news."

Magazines began again to beg Takami for manuscripts. For well over a year, he had not been asked to write anything, but publishers now were sending people every day to his house. On September 21, he wrote, "Kamiyama of *Shinjoen* came to see me for the third time. He is desperately anxious for me to write a story thirty *mai* long. I had made up my mind not to write any more magazine articles, but it is hard suddenly to break an old connection."[30]

There was a flood of new magazines. Most lasted no more than three issues, at which point the rampant inflation had so diminished the value of the publishers' funds that they had no choice but to cease publication. The failure of one after another magazine did not discourage prospective publishers, each of whom believed there was a public waiting for a new and slightly different magazine. They counted on the general craving for reading matter, at a time when there was little other entertainment that most people could afford.

Regardless of the nature of a magazine, stories or articles by well-known writers were essential to attracting prospective readers. Takami greatly benefited by the extraordinary attention he received, but his gratitude was mixed with annoyance about the importunities of the publishers, and he grew quite furious when he listed the changed titles of wartime magazines, evidence of the publishers' pandering to postwar tastes:

Weapons and Technology is now *Peace Industries*; *Nippon Deutsch-land* is now *Nippon America*; *Navy Report* is now *Story*. I burst out laughing, but my laughter soon faded away. What shameless audacity! What fickleness! What arrogance! I laughed because it was so extremely stupid, but it was also so shameful my laughter could not last long. This is not confined to magazines. It's emblematic of the internal corruption of Japan, a country that could not but lose the war. It's a typical example of the stupidity of the Japanese. As long as such things are permitted, with no consideration of the feelings of the people, Japan is doomed. Democracy will never amount to anything.[31]

Takami's irritation over the flip-flops of publishers was excessive, but it typified his overwrought reactions to anything he disliked at this time. On September 29, a sarcastic remark by his mother, followed by her complaints about one thing or another, aroused uncontrollable anger. He slapped her. "This was the first time in my life I have done such a thing," he wrote. The next morning, the quarrel with his mother resumed and almost resulted in blows:

My squabbles with my mother are repeated again and again, never ending. They are followed by intense remorse, but they never stop. This was the first time, however, they reached such violence. I happened to be in the kitchen when I was carrying on, and I scattered rice all over the place. Precious rice. Last night I scattered a little rice over the living room. . . . An accursed mother and son. —The feeling is really profound.

My wife started to shriek, and called in a loud voice to Nakamura-san [a neighbor], asking for help. He rushed in and restrained my mother, who was distraught. I was also in a complete frenzy. I thought I would kill my mother and then myself. This happens every time.

Thinking about my work rescued me from my frenzy. If I didn't have my work, I'd have long since killed myself.

Come to think of it, this endless family discord was for me the most important question, the question that always tormented me the most. And yet I have never tried to treat this most important question in my work.[32]

On October 4, Takami read Molière's *Le Misanthrope*. Perhaps he had a reason for reading this particular play. It may even have inspired him to turn from society to himself: "Up to now I have never written about myself, but now I am interested only in myself. I think I shall write a history of the development of my mentality [*seishin*]." The next day, he wrote,

I was in my study until two in the morning working on the outline of my novel. I felt my excitement gradually welling up. I want to write about the ten years that were like a bad dream. How during the ten years people lived, how they writhed in order to live, and how the ten years tormented people, wounded them, distorted them, killed them. This is what I want to write. I want to write these things focusing on myself. I want to sculpt my own image, which will also be a representative portrait. The time has arrived for me to throw myself into my work and write about what I truly want to write![33]

Although various political organizations were founded immediately after the war, taking advantage of the new freedom, Takami was not tempted to join any of them or to write works that would further political causes:

I've had enough of politics. I've had enough of political action. I've had enough of groups. I've had enough of party factions.

Before long there probably will be a flood of "political novels," "group novels," "party-faction novels." I welcome the appearance of such works because they will help to rescue Japanese literature from its present poverty, but I shall be upset if they are not good as literature. I shall be upset if, thanks to the strength of political groups or factions, nonliterary works swagger about wearing the face of literature. And I am sure they will swagger. In this manner, a new authority will come into being for the oppression of literature.[34]

Takami had come to realize that he wanted to write about himself, tracing his incessantly repeated avowals of shame to its origin. As a child, he had lived in a Tokyo slum with his mother, who did piecework sewing to supplement the meager allowance sent by Takami's father, the former governor of Fukui Prefecture, who refused even to look at his illegitimate son. Takami's mother had given him a strict upbringing, no doubt in order to make him into a gentleman, despite his birth. But gossip about the mother and son led to the taunts of neighbors. When Takami was about to take the entrance examination for the most prestigious middle school in Tokyo, a classmate informed him (maliciously and incorrectly) that illegitimate boys were not admitted to that school. Takami declared in a novel that the news made him hate his mother, holding her responsible for the shame.[35] But her piecework sewing continued until he had safely obtained a university degree.

In his diary entry for February 12, 1946, Takami wrote, "I have begun to write *Aru tamashii no kokuhaku* [*Confessions of a Soul*]. I am writing as though possessed." In the March issue of *Shinchō*, he published the first episode of a new novel, *Waga mune no soko no koko ni wa* (*Here, in the Depths of My Heart*).[36] The novel, which was intended to describe his boyhood and early manhood, was never completed. Perhaps Takami found it painful to recount boyhood experiences of shame, the dominant theme, but the direction of his future work had been set. His novels from this time on would not be fiction about the denizens of Asakusa but revelations of himself, though in many guises.

Takami's novels, written both before and after the war, had many admirers. Critics spoke of "the age of Takami Jun." His diary is even more impressive than his novels. Many entries are no longer of interest, and the lengthy newspaper articles he pasted into the diary require patience to read, but the whole not only paints a picture of an era but gives unforgettable details and vignettes. Takami's account of a train ride from Kamakura to Tokyo on October 5, 1945, coming as it does after many harsh appraisals of the Japanese, is striking for his discovery of a Japanese for whom he felt respect, a young officer:

I took the 2:13 train to Tokyo.

It was fairly empty. At Yokohama, several black soldiers came aboard and began to talk in loud voices. Roars of laughter. Finally, with no concern for anybody else, they began to lark about.... Annoyed, I deliberately refrained from looking at them, but they were making such a commotion that I inadvertently looked in their direction. It was then that I noticed a young Japanese officer sitting near these black soldiers whose uproarious laughter bared white teeth that contrasted with the blackness of their faces. Something about the Japanese struck me. When I looked more carefully, I saw he was wearing an officer's overcoat with gold buttons and officer's boots. His uniform was that of an officer, but the star insignia on his cap had been removed. He had been demobilized. No doubt he had gone from the university into the army and become a first or second lieutenant. His face was that of an intellectual.

What must he have felt as he watched the scarcely human behavior of the black soldiers? Imagining what he must be feeling, I felt I could not look him squarely in the face.

But, a bit worried, I stole a glance. A quiet smile was playing on the officer's face. It was not a sneer. And, of course, it was not a servile smile or a forced smile. It was a completely natural smile. He had been led to smile naturally by the innocent antics of the black soldiers.

I felt relieved. No, I felt thankful.

I really felt a kind of gratitude that such a Japanese exists, that such a mild-mannered Japanese had been called up for compulsory military service and had been an officer. There are such Japanese. There had even been such officers. To exaggerate somewhat, I had been rescued from despair. That was how I felt. I was able, thanks to him, to think of the entire Japanese people as a

fine people—mild-mannered, easy-going, basically not at all bel-
ligerent. I felt saved. —That's the kind of feeling it was. I was certain that such an officer would have been courageous on the battlefield, not a coward but a splendid hero. —There was even such
excellence in the Japanese people.

A beautiful young woman was sitting beside the demobilized
officer. They got off together at Shinagawa. Probably they were a
young couple. I prayed for their happiness.[37]

Takami in his diary again and again expressed despair about the
Japanese. He had seen officers in China behaving unspeakably and had
contempt for those who, once the war had ended, had shifted without
transition from worship of the emperor to servility toward the Americans. But the smile of the young officer, a quiet smile that showed pleasure at seeing people enjoying themselves, though in an egregiously
un-Japanese manner, gave Takami hope for the Japanese.

The same day, a friend showed Takami a copy of *Life* with a photograph of Benito Mussolini's naked corpse hanging upside down from a
tree, together with the corpse of his mistress. Takami found it too horrible to look at: "I was no admirer of Mussolini. I, in fact, sympathized
with the Italian partisans in their hatred of Mussolini. But such sav-
agery. . . . I believe that the hatred of the Japanese people for Tōjō was
no less intense than that of the partisans for Mussolini. But the Japanese did not drag Tōjō from his house and lynch him."

Takami said to a friend, "The Japanese are gentle, aren't they?" "Like
little lambs," answered the friend. Takami commented in his diary,

That's right. The Japanese in some respects have been emascu-
lated. In some ways, the reign of terror turned them into little
lambs incapable of expressing openly their anger in either words
or deeds—spiritless, strengthless human beings. But one can't
say that their failure to hang Tōjō upside down proves that, unlike the Italians, they are a gentle people who dislike cruelty.

Even the Japanese were cruel. It might be more accurate to say
that the Japanese were particularly cruel. The Japanese soldiers

at the front in China indulged in acts of cruelty to their heart's content.

The Japanese become cruel when they have power. When their power is taken away, they are docile as lambs, even servile. What cowardice this is! But this also was the case because every kind of power had been taken from the hands of the common people. So when they were given power, they wanted to display it. They became inhuman. They became brutal. They overstepped the bounds. It was a kind of hysteria induced by the fact that power had never before been placed in their hands. The poor Japanese.[38]

On October 6, he read that, by command of the Occupation headquarters, all political prisoners were to be released from jail and that the Tokkō Keisatsu (Special Secret Service Police) had been abolished. He wrote in his diary,

I felt tremendously relieved, as if dark clouds had been cleared. But why did we have to wait for the command to come from Allied Headquarters? Why couldn't we do it ourselves? I feel ashamed. If we had done it with our own hands, my happiness would be much deeper, and there would not be this feeling of shame at the bottom of my happiness.[39]

Two weeks later, Takami visited the house of a friend from high-school days, Uchino Sōji, a Communist. A party was held to celebrate Uchino's release from prison on October 10 as the result of the American order to free political prisoners. As he walked toward Uchino's house, Takami recalled that if the war had not ended two months earlier, he could not have attended the party without the gravest fears. The party would have had to be held under the watchful eyes of the Special Secret Service Police; if it had been attempted to throw a party without their authorization, the perpetrator would have been arrested. Just to be seen at such a gathering would have invited denunciation by someone present, even if he were a friend; individual friendships were not recognized. The change in two months had been immense. Almost every day something irritated Takami, whether the sight of a Japanese woman consorting with an American soldier or a Japanese man fawning over the conquerors. But the Special Secret Service Police had been abolished. Takami was no longer afraid.

DURING THE MONTHS after the defeat of Japan, men who had been released from military service or work in munitions plants were obliged to search for other jobs in order to feed themselves and their families. The prospects were bleak, and some even died of starvation. It took years for unemployment to be reduced and for inflation to be brought under control. Recollections of the immediate postwar period are therefore almost always gloomy, but these years nevertheless saw an extraordinary revitalization of Japanese culture in almost every field.

Writers who had been silenced by the military or who had not wished to publish the expected patriotic effusions regained their voices and were now besieged for stories and articles by the editors of innumerable new magazines. They welcomed the beginning of a new era and the freedom to express themselves without fear. Few voiced despair over the defeat or hope that Japan would soon take its revenge. Instead, the defeat, the prospect of which had inspired such horror that some believed death was preferable, was taken in their stride by most Japanese. Their thoughts were directed toward the future. Far from expressing bitterness about the loss of Japan's overseas possessions, they were proud that the new constitution made Japan the first country to renounce the possession of an army or a navy. There were many occasions for complaint and even confrontation during the Occupation, but not for years would any writer express nostalgia for the martial triumphs of imperial Japan.

Most authors could hardly wait to start writing again. Only a few, like Uchida Hyakken, chose not to publish; almost every page of his diary for 1946 mentions his rejection of a request for a manuscript. He did not give his reasons. Perhaps he felt that it was still too early to write the "positive" articles that most magazines desired.

Takami Jun, who a few months earlier had so few requests for manuscripts that he considered taking a job on a cattle farm, spent the night of October 23, 1945, writing letters to four periodicals refusing their requests for articles and stories. He explained, "I breathe more easily, now that I have become accustomed to freedom, but at the same time, everything that catches my attention makes me unbearably angry. And I am angry also with myself. I feel excruciatingly ashamed of what I have done up to now. I have fallen into a state of not wanting to write anything."[1]

One cause of his anger was the readiness of Japanese women to consort with American soldiers. This was, of course, a source of irritation and even humiliation for most Japanese men, not only writers. Some of these women were prostitutes, happy to ply their trade with moneyed customers. Other women merely hoped to be taken to dinner or to ride in a jeep. Still others seem to have turned away from Japanese men because of the defeat and found that the victors were kinder to women. Takami's reaction, typically, was a feeling of shame. In October 1945, he recorded in his diary an incident observed one evening at a Tokyo train station. It was getting dark and there were no electric lights:

> I could see a crowd of people on the opposite platform. There were sounds of laughter. I wondered if the laughter came from some drunken American soldiers. They were saying something in loud voices and making comic gestures. Japanese, including two young female station attendants, had clustered around them. The American soldiers were pointing to a place beside them, indicating that the women should come closer. They went on making these gestures. The Japanese men around them were laughing uproariously. The two women with attitudes of "Ohh—I don't want to" were hugging each other coquettishly. They looked as if being flirted with this way was unbearably pleasurable.
>
> Another woman station attendant came up. Everything about her suggested that she also wanted to be teased. What an indescribably shameful sight! I was appalled by the thought that these disgraceful women would have the right to vote. And the men watching on in amusement had lower intelligence than South Pacific natives.
>
> Japanese culture, to be absolutely frank, was on the same low level as in the colonies of the South Pacific. The Japanese had too high an opinion of themselves. I also had too high an opinion of myself.[2]

The sight of Japanese men, eager to ingratiate themselves and to do business with their recent enemies, also exasperated Takami. He described a scene he witnessed on October 29. A Japanese in blue work clothes, sidling up to an American soldier, said, "*Harō, shigaretto.*" Takami professed to have difficulty understanding what the man was trying to say: "*Harō* is 'hello,' but *shigaretto* is not 'cigarette.' His pronunciation was quite peculiar. *Shiga* must be Shiga Prefecture, and *retto* is *rettō*, 'inferior.' What he was saying was 'Hello! Shiga is inferior.'" This, obviously, was *not* the man's meaning. Although expressed humorously, Takami's contempt is clear. Such Japanese seemed to have lost all pride. Nearby, at the entrance to Shinbashi Station, was another depressing sight—juvenile vagrants sleeping on the pavement. No doubt they had been orphaned by the war.[3]

Yamada Fūtarō recorded that when children saw a jeep passing by, they cried "Banzai!" again and again: "The American soldiers scatter chocolates and cigarettes, and not only children but adults crawl about picking them up. The Americans open their big mouths and laugh." He heard that American soldiers went into department stores and carried off merchandise, leaving in exchange one cigarette: "When they are riding in their jeeps, they make a great commotion whenever they see a woman and wave their hands. An ordinary woman will turn pale and run away, but I hear women from the licensed quarter now walk hand-in-hand with them in Honmoku."[4]

Although Yamada was reluctant to admit that there was anything to praise in the conduct of the Americans, he noted that when a Japanese officer was brought to court, charged with killing three American soldiers who had broken into his house intending to rob him, the court ruled that this was a legitimate act of self-defense, and the Japanese was immediately released.[5] Yamada gradually moved away somewhat from his professed hatred. Although he continued to refer to the Americans as "the enemy," by the end of September 1945 he was writing,

> I hear that enemy military police officers treat people in an extremely fair manner, and that the Occupation, considering it is being carried out by a victorious army, is going extremely well. This is because the present Occupation force consists of picked troops. Besides, Japan has not yet been totally disarmed and the enemy is afraid of the Japanese. (Japanese swords, whether carried by the military or civilians, seem to be what the enemy dreads most. Might a drawn-sword attack[6] be effective?) The enemy cites acts of atrocity performed by Japanese forces in China and the Philippines, but if one stops to think, were not the Chinese and the Filipinos the peoples who resisted the Japanese most determinedly? It wasn't true of Indonesia or Burma. Besides, it was in the midst of fierce fighting, quite a different thing from the

solemn, silent welcome that greeted the enemy when he landed in Japan.[7]

Yamada, puzzled by the good behavior of the Occupation troops, decided that they were special—the pride of the American army, quite unlike the mass of American soldiers. His intuitions (as in this case) tended to be groundless, but he questioned not only the behavior of the enemy but the beliefs for which the Japanese had fought. When a friend asked Yamada why the Japanese, whenever anyone mentioned *Nippon seishin* (Japanese spirit), now gave contemptuous laughs and changed the subject, he replied,

> People have come to be prejudiced against *Nippon seishin* because of the heaven-sent, illogical, self-righteous attitude of its enthusiasts in the past. Take, for example, the Divine Oracle [*shinchoku*].[8] They claimed that it was absolute and signified that the Land of the Gods will never perish.   ·
>
> But what is the Divine Oracle anyway? I believe it was something like an imperial edict, first proclaimed by an ancestor of the present emperor. The ancestor, needless to say, was a human being. It was rather like Hitler's screaming the certainty of a German victory. But why is it absolute? And why should the Land of the Gods be immortal because of this oracle? When the time comes for Japan to perish, it will perish.
>
> And what is meant by the Land of the Gods? It is good to have pride in the land of one's ancestors, and perhaps it is necessary. "Land of the Gods" may be a suitably poetic expression useful in arousing patriotic emotions, but how was it possible for people to be so self-possessed that they blindly invoked the immortality of the Land of the Gods and linked our destiny to this one expression? And is it not ludicrous for us to speak ill of the Jews for believing they are the chosen people?

At this point, Yamada's friend asked sarcastically if he was about to transfer to the "democracy bus." He answered,

Why do you look at me with that sneer on your face? That's not what I'm saying. To tell the truth, I don't know what democracy is. For that matter, we Japanese were not taught what Communism is either. All we were taught, quite categorically, is that it's very, very bad. But what's bad about it? We haven't got the slightest idea. Maybe it really is bad. But what makes it so? Are we not permitted to have any doubts about its badness? Isn't it quite natural for a human being to doubt? I would like to adopt the attitude of the medical men of modern times who started from basic doubts about the medicine of Aristotle and Galen. This may make you angry, but I doubt even the existence of *Nippon seishin* itself. . . .

I respect and love His Majesty the Emperor, but I dislike those who make a business out of their respect. And, to tell the truth, I would not die spiritually even if there were no emperor. I believe that the majority of Japanese would probably not die. That's because there are so many pleasures to live for.[9]

On October 1, Yamada wrote,

During the war we were taught that Japan, the Land of the Gods, was a righteous, divine country and that America was an evil, barbaric country. We didn't actually believe this, but merely followed along, thinking that, since there was no such thing as a just war, such poisonous, simple-minded rhetoric was a convenient way to whip up a state of furious belligerence in the people.

Again, we had doubts as to whether or not Japan would be capable after the war of guiding the Greater East Asia Co-Prosperity Sphere. (We did not think we would be defeated. It was not that we were so convinced of victory that we never thought of defeat. It was simply unbearable to contemplate it, and because we could not imagine what our fate would be afterward, we shielded our eyes from the possibility and went on believing in certain victory.) But just supposing we won the war, we doubted whether the Japanese would do a better job than the Anglo-Saxons, the Soviets, the Germans, and the Italians had done in leading their respective Co-Prosperity Spheres.

This was not simply a matter of scientific or cultural strength. We felt uneasy with respect to our inborn capacity as human beings. This, in the final analysis, was due to the wretched insularism of the Japanese. But we thought that if somehow or other we could win the present war, and somehow or other managed to establish the Greater East Asia Co-Prosperity Sphere, competition with other advanced countries would polish us. Our insularism would be swept away, and the magnanimity of a large-minded, great people would be cultivated.

People of the future will find it strange that during the war we so easily accepted an education smacking of distorted self-esteem and hostility that advocated such preposterous ambitions, but for us the reasons seemed compelling.[10]

In the October 2 issue of the *Mainichi shinbun*, Yamada read the article "The Dark Age Has Ended" by the novelist Ishikawa Tatsuzō, in which he begged General Douglas MacArthur to reign over Japan as long as possible ("even one day longer") in order to beat into shape the spiritual outlook of present-day Japanese.[11] Yamada, calling this an irresponsible, shallow piece of writing, criticized Ishikawa in these terms:

Was he not one of the popular Japanese authors of the day who during the war wrote innumerable war stories, essays, and poems and with them influenced to some degree the minds of the Japanese masses? Was he not one of those who, when the war broke out, raised shouts of joy and admiration for Japanese soldiers, saying they were the matchless romanticists of all times and all nations?

He's one of the Japanese who should be whipped. Now, when there is a contemptible tendency to assign to the military entire responsibility for the war, should writers, the first to be infected by this tendency, be forgiven? Think of the men who have died![12]

Ishikawa's expressed reverence for General MacArthur resembled that of the Japanese Communists who, believing that MacArthur was sympathetic to their cause, presented for his action a list of writers whom they denounced as war criminals deserving of punishment. Ishikawa urged MacArthur to be extremely stringent in dealing with those responsible for having led Japan into the war.

This was not easy. So many authors had eagerly cooperated with the war effort that it would have been difficult to single out those who merited being imprisoned or at the very least ostracized. Only senior writers like Nagai Kafū and Tanizaki Jun'ichirō had totally escaped involvement with the military. They were too old to be called up for military service, and, thanks to royalties from their books, they were not obliged to write propaganda in order to survive. Most writers felt that they had had no choice but to cooperate with the war effort, at least to the extent of joining the Bunpō. Takami Jun recalled the previous ten years as a nightmare, but he, no less than Ishikawa Tatsuzō, had written in praise of the war.

Accusations of collaboration with the militarists were likely to be met with counter-charges. Few writers were ready to admit that their impassioned support of the war had been a serious mistake of judgment. The poet Takamura Kōtarō was perhaps the most striking example. He had been passionately convinced of the justice of the war and had never doubted that Japan would be victorious. Even after the surrender, he declared in a poem that if the emperor's person were threatened, the entire Japanese population would die in the effort to protect him:

Sanctity must not be violated.
We Japanese, surrounding that one Man,
Will form a wall of people manifold in depth.
If anyone tries to lay a finger on that Sanctity,
We Japanese, without exception, will lay down side by side
And defend Him to our last extremity.[13]

His readiness to die for the emperor seemed a basic part of Takamura's patriotism, but by 1947, in "Shūsen" (End of the War), his attitude began to change:

> We were saved from starvation by the Occupation Army,
> And barely escaped with our lives.
> At that time the emperor himself came forward
> And declared he was not a living god.
> With the passage of time
> The beam was removed from my eye;
> Before I knew it, a heavy weight of sixty years had melted away.[14]

Takamura was tormented especially by fear that his poetry, which had glorified the war, might have caused the deaths of many men. This was the subject of his poem "Wa ga shi wo yomite hito shi ni tsukeri" (Men, Having Read My Poems, Went to Their Deaths):

> To save myself from the fear of death,
> I became desperate about the "desperate times" and wrote.
> My countrymen at the front lines read these poems.
> Men read them and went to their deaths.
> The submarine captain who wrote his family
> That he reread my poems each day soon afterward went down
>   with his ship.[15]

Saitō Mokichi (1882–1953), revered as the most distinguished tanka poet of the twentieth century, had been passionately committed to the war. After the war, he punished himself for his mistake by sequestering himself in a small town in Yamagata Prefecture. Other poets, passing over their wartime effusions in silence, attempted to expunge all remembrance of them by not including them in postwar collections of their works.

Many writers at this time wrote prophecies of how the defeat would change Japan. Yamada Fūtarō 's prophecies were among the most accurate:

At the rate things are going, extreme adulation of America will increasingly sweep over Japan. Harsh criticism of the military will be rampant—so much whipping of the dead. To a certain extent this may be necessary, and there is likely to be a period when novels and criticism will consist of shallow, hysterical exposures for the sake of exposure. And will this in turn be followed by another period of self-examination? —The world is really stupid.[16]

Others, though at first far more enthusiastic than Yamada about the reforms ordered by the American Occupation authorities, before long became critical, mainly as the result of the censorship that was initiated in September 1945. The ostensible purpose of this censorship was to eliminate militarism, the cause of the war. Any expression of admiration in literature, old or new, for such traditional Japanese virtues as loyalty and filial piety was regarded with suspicion and condemned as feudalistic. When a woman was praised in a play in the traditional manner as "a good wife and wise mother," this wording was considered by the American censors as a feudalistic denial of women's right to lead independent lives. Above all, anything suggestive of martial glory was taboo.

By this time, most Japanese were thoroughly disillusioned with the military, and few would have objected to the total elimination of militarism from textbooks or literature. But the censors, with traditional stupidity, went beyond the stated purpose of the censorship. They prohibited books that were not militaristic, often for inadequate or even absurd reasons. An inconsequential story by Tanizaki Jun'ichirō could not be published because it describes the childish admiration of a woman for a pilot she has never met. She is so entranced with him that she supposes that his plane flies more gracefully than do the others in his squadron and that its engine emits musical sounds instead of the usual roar. The censors decided that the story was a covert expression of militarism and banned its publication in 1946. It was printed in 1950, by which time the American censors were working with different guidelines.[17]

An egregious instance of censorship was directed in 1946 at the film *Nihon no higeki* (*A Japanese Tragedy*). This documentary was made with the encouragement of the chief American censor, who hoped that it would help eliminate militarism and democratize Japan. Newsreels and similar sources were used in the film to show how the emperor, the militarists, the politicians, and the intellectuals had glorified the war, and to reveal the huge profits capitalists had made at a time when many Japanese were suffering from hunger. The film was passed by the American censors with minor deletions and was shown at small theaters (the larger ones rejected it because it was too gloomy), but a second censorship review found the film objectionable and prohibited it on the grounds that its implication that the emperor had started the war with the United States might cause offended Japanese to riot. The Americans now believed that the cooperation of the emperor was essential to the success of the Occupation.[18]

Japanese censors both before and during the war had suppressed offensive words in works of literature, replacing them with XX or OO. But perceptive readers could guess, for example, that XXX stood for Kyō-san-tō, the Communist Party. Passages were censored not only in newly written works but in the classics. The novels of Ihara Saikaku (1642–1693) appeared with words or sentences deemed to be pornographic rendered as strings of crosses or circles. A more serious instance was the censorship of Tanizaki's modern-language translation of *The Tale of Genji*. Permission to print was granted only after he deleted offending chapters—those relating how a prince, born of Genji's affair with the emperor's consort, had ascended the throne as emperor.[19]

Occupation censors did not permit the use of XX or OO because they would call attention to deletions of words or paragraphs. They insisted that offending passages be rewritten completely, in order to eliminate the traces of censorship.

Despite the many instances of narrow-mindedness, if not foolishness, that might be cited, the Occupation censors believed that they were helping the Japanese along the road to democracy. Their censorship was by no means as severe as prewar and wartime Japanese censorship, but American censorship, even if its purpose was laudable, contradicted freedom of the press, an ideal often proclaimed by the Americans. Despite the irritating censorship, there was no danger (as had been true when the censors were Japanese) that an author or editor would be imprisoned for a violation of the publication code. The censorship was a source of frustration, but it did not keep authors from publishing a remarkable body of literature.

A dazzling array of writers was active at this time. Some with established reputations, like Tanizaki and Kawabata Yasunari, continued to produce important works. Dazai Osamu (1909–1948) and Mishima Yukio (1925–1970), who had earlier attracted attention with one or two books, first gained wide recognition during the Occupation era. Dazai's fiction, notably *Bion no tsuma* (*Villon's Wife*) and *Shayō* (*The Setting Sun*), both published in 1947, established his reputation as the most gifted portraitist of postwar Japan. Mishima's *Kamen no kokuhaku* (*Confessions of a Mask*, 1949) revealed a major new voice. Still other major figures, like Abe Kōbō, began to publish at this time. Shiga Naoya, who had lapsed into silence, began to write again, and Nagai Kafū produced several volumes of short stories. Has there ever been a time in the history of Japanese literature when so many important authors were writing?

Recollections of the war years, some of permanent interest, began to appear almost as soon as the war ended. A noteworthy feature of the new writing was the revival of specifically left-wing literature after the long period of suppression. Noma Hiroshi's *Shinkū chitai* (*Zone of Emptiness*, 1952), a realistic account of life in the Japanese army during the war, was acclaimed by many critics as the great modern Japanese novel. It was included in lists of the hundred best novels of the world.

Readers were excited by the flood of new works, but now that the defeat had called into question the value of Japanese culture, they also wanted badly to discover what, if anything, they could be proud of in their past. People waited in line all night to be sure of getting a copy of a volume from the collected works of the philosopher Nishida Kitarō. They hoped to find in his writing, far too difficult for the average person to understand, reassurance that Japanese thought, traditional or not, was of value.

Japanese authors were nevertheless ready to discard tradition. Many poets ceased to compose haiku after Kuwabara Takeo, a professor of French literature at Kyoto University, declared in 1946 that haiku was no more than a second-class art, proving his point by asking people to judge haiku with the name of the poet concealed. The results were so chaotic that Kuwabara believed there was no real standard of excellence in haiku, only a respect for famous poets.

The defeat also made artists want to break out of the bounds of traditional Japanese painting and to experiment with the latest trends in art elsewhere. Exhibitions of European art, the first since before the war, attracted immense crowds, and few young artists were interested in learning the techniques of Japanese painting. Each new wave in Western art had ripples in Japan.

Theater had flourished during the war years, but after the war ended, the survival of the three major forms of traditional Japanese drama— Nō, Bunraku, and Kabuki—became uncertain, partly because people were tired of the wartime insistence on the superiority of pure Japanese art to the commercial theater of the West. Kabuki, it is true, was still popular, but its survival was threatened by the decision of the Occupation authorities to prohibit plays that might serve to revive feudalistic beliefs. This decree removed many of the finest works from the repertory.[20] Bunraku was equally affected by the ban on feudalistic plays, and though performances were of exceptionally high quality, the Bunraku theater in Osaka was often nearly empty.

Nō actors commonly predicted the doom of their art, sure that its slow pace and difficult language were anathema to young Japanese infatuated with the new culture. Kyōgen, which shared stages with Nō as comic relief, should have fared better, but probably no more than ten men in the whole country made a living as Kyōgen actors. The Japanese seemed to be on the point of jettisoning their heritage in the theater arts. This did not happen, but it took time before the traditional theater could reclaim its place in a culture where the modernism it shared with the rest of the world had come to seem crucially important.

Far greater interest was shown in modern theater (*shingeki*). The enormous popularity of *Yūzuru* (*Twilight Crane*, 1947) by Kinoshita

Junji (1914–2006) encouraged those who worried about the survival of Japanese traditions. This play, based on authentic folk materials, appealed to audiences because it was at once modern and traditional, Japanese and yet universally appealing. The modern theater in Japan had been created as far back as the beginning of the twentieth century, but only in the postwar era did it become a integral part of Japanese cultural life.

Films of every kind remained extremely popular with the general public. Historical subjects were avoided because the Occupation officials frowned on the idealization of the Japanese past, but kissing and near pornography on the screen were tolerated.

At an even more popular level than films, the comedies of Furukawa Roppa (1903–1961) brought cheer to the Japanese during the dark postwar days. Roppa's diary, a minutely detailed account of his daily life and his activity in the theater, gives a quite different view of the Occupation from those found in diaries kept by professional writers, most of whom were able to go about their work without concerning themselves with the Occupation authorities. But Roppa had to establish good relations with the Americans; their permission was needed before he could stage a performance.

The Americans were happy to meet Roppa. Although they could not understand the Japanese dialogue, they enjoyed the singing and dancing in his plays. Roppa's company, thanks to the friends he made, was never subjected to the pressure that Shōchiku, a much bigger theatrical organization, suffered during the Occupation.

Roppa's American friends were generous with canned goods, cigarettes, and other luxuries not available to most Japanese. At a time of a serious food shortage, Roppa, who devoted considerable attention in his diary to describing his meals, usually ate quite well. Hoping to further improve his relations with Occupation personnel, he attempted to memorize an English dictionary, but never got beyond the letter A. One of his popular songs was called "Do You Speak English?", and he learned from Occupation soldiers such classics as "Alexander's Ragtime Band" and "Rum and Coca-Cola."

Roppa's performances, whether in Tokyo or in provincial towns, were generally well attended. There were hardships: because most theaters in Tokyo had been destroyed in the bombing, he often had no choice but to perform on unsuitable stages. Elsewhere in the country, theaters often had only primitive facilities. His performances also faced severe competition. He told his company, "Your biggest enemy is not the established companies but American movies. Unless you can challenge them, you'll never make a success."[21] The popularity of American films, shown for the first time since 1941, was also a threat to Japanese films, most of them produced hastily at minimal expense. No one could have expected the worldwide triumph of Kurosawa Akira's *Rashōmon* in 1950.

Roppa did not hesitate to criticize the Occupation. He described in his diary, for example, how on a streetcar an American soldier had offered him ten packs of Chesterfields for ¥350. This was rather high—the going price for a pack was ¥30—but Roppa bought the cigarettes anyway, though he felt embarrassed about dealing with a black marketeer. The soldier then offered him a can of beef and vegetable stew for ¥50 that Roppa also bought, this time feeling a kind of self-hatred.[22]

On November 11, 1945, Roppa received the good news that Japanese controls on the theater had been lifted and it was no longer necessary to report to the police.[23] This relief did not last long: instead, the even more taxing requirement of obtaining prior approval from the Occupation authorities was imposed. A summary of the work to be performed had to be submitted in advance, and not until it was approved could the writing of the script begin. Every word of the scenario had to be translated into English and a typed copy submitted.

On the same day, Roppa noted in his diary that the Occupation troops had staged what he called a "cowboy show." He heard the rumor that the horse on which the emperor used to ride would take part. Roppa, remembering awe-inspiring photographs of the emperor on the horse, felt a painful awareness of what defeat meant.[24]

On January 1, 1946, Roppa's New Year celebration was distinctly low-key. He did not bother to wear a formal kimono, and at breakfast there was none of the traditional food or the spiced saké. When he left his house, he saw no flags or pine boughs at people's doors. The tram was emptier than usual. Roppa got off downtown, at Yūraku-chō. Americans and their wives were strolling there. The newspapers that day carried a photograph of the emperor in a business suit and depictions of the empress's private quarters. Roppa was saddened by the loss of the aura that had surrounded the imperial family.[25] He failed to mention that the emperor, in a radio broadcast on the same day, had denied his divinity. This announcement probably made Roppa even sadder.

A few weeks later, he heard a radio broadcast of the emperor's visit to a factory. Roppa commented, "It is somehow painful to hear His Majesty the Emperor's voice so often, and the presentation was terrible. It was a role too difficult even for His Majesty the Emperor to perform. I felt sorry for him. All he said was, 'Ah, so. Ah, so.'"[26]

On January 19, the evening newspaper reported that Kabuki was dead: it had been totally banned by order of Supreme Commander of the Allied Powers. Roppa commented,

> The Americans' lack of understanding of art is lamentable. It isn't as bad as what the Japanese have done, but, in any case, it is unwarranted. One might say it was Shōchiku's fault. Their lack of planning and stupidity invited this consequence. Uzaemon was lucky to have died when he did. I can imagine what Kikugorō and the other Kabuki actors must be going through. It is the misery of a defeated country that such a thing has followed so quickly on the destruction of our geography and history. After getting into bed, I wrote the second installment of "Roppa's English Lessons" for *Style*. Writing went well, and I managed to write ten *mai*.[27]

Roppa frequently went on tour. One-night stops were grueling, especially when he performed before unresponsive audiences, but it was a pleasure to return to Kyoto, which remained mercifully undamaged. In Atami, on the way home, he had excellent meals and was delighted that the shops were again well stocked with souvenirs. Japan seemed to be returning to prewar prosperity, but on returning to Tokyo, Roppa's first impressions were of "American soldiers, Negroes, and the shameful lipsticks of the Japanese women clinging to them."[28]

Roppa's profession was to make people laugh, but the tone of his diary, reflecting the uncertainty of the time, is seldom cheerful. All the same, there were signs of improvement in daily life, and the world of culture was bursting with energy. Despite the paper shortage and the wartime destruction of printing facilities, the publication of books rebounded. Ten times as many books were published in May as in January 1946. Over half the new books were reprints of prewar works.[29] The 1930s were by no means a golden age of Japanese democracy, but books of that period, compared with those of the war years, reassured readers that militarism had not always been dominant. The Occupation era seemed (to some at least) like a resumption of traditions that had been brutally interrupted by the war.

Everything connected with the war was now hateful or shaming. Roppa explained why he was reluctant to sing a song that had been popular during the war: "If I found it distasteful, I felt sure the audience would sense this. I didn't want to see or hear anything from wartime."[30]

THE MOST detailed and vivid diary of the early Occupation period is undoubtedly Takami Jun's. He wrote an entry every day, some of them reaching more than ten pages in length. He also cut articles from newspapers and pasted them into the diary to provide details on events he had reported. It must have seemed an unending task, and occasionally he asked himself if keeping the diary was worth the trouble and was giving him real satisfaction:

> I wonder how many pages of manuscript paper this diary comes to. I'm surprised I've managed to write so much. It's become quite a major "work."

A "work"? —There's not much joy in this one. I wonder why. Cézanne in his letter to Emile Zola of May 20, 1881, wrote, "I hope you will soon recover your normal state in your work. I think that, despite all the alternatives, *work is the sole refuge where one can find true satisfaction.*"[1]

Mine brings no such satisfaction. Or joy. In any case, this diary doesn't count as a "work." It's hardly even an étude. Supposing one writes some stupid piece of popular fiction (though this would not count as a "work" either), one can feel joy when it is finished. This may be self-deception or self-hallucination, but it is the joy of creation. And there is satisfaction. . . .

I can't find that writing a diary brings even that much satisfaction. There's no joy in it. No, perhaps I had some while the war was still going on. I have forgotten. But now, even after having written a considerable number of pages of diary, I do not derive from them as much joy as I might experience after writing one stupid story. I may have been able to find self-satisfaction in the diary while writing during the war, but this has fizzled out completely. I am writing merely out of habit. A sad habit. I am writing as if it were a painful duty. And, having kept writing this far, it would be a waste to break it off now. That seems to be my frame of mind as I write. . . .

During the war, I continued to write this diary assiduously, never knowing when it might go up in flames. When the war entered the "decisive battle for the homeland" phase, I made up my mind to take the diary with me if I were evacuated. I realized that if I fell somewhere along the way, the diary might get smeared with dirt; it might rot. I was well aware of this, but I continued to write diligently, knowing it might be in vain. Was my fervor aroused by awareness of how likely the diary was to perish?

Now I have no such worries. As long as my house doesn't catch fire, the diary is safe. It will remain. I shall leave it for the future. It is worthy of being called a "work."

But although I think in these terms, I can no longer feel the same ardor.[2]

Three weeks later, Takami wrote, "I am writing this diary entirely for myself, but I wonder if can be made into a work that satisfies me. The one thing certain is that it's not something written for other people."[3] Toward the end of 1945, pondering the value of the diary, he rebuked himself:

> I must keep this diary more faithfully, as faithfully as I did in the past. A time will surely come when I shall be glad to have written down even things that now seem inconsequential. So I tell myself, but once I get started on a piece of writing, I have trouble keeping up the diary. It's because of my work that the diary has of late become short-winded and careless, but I must keep at it, even when pursued by deadlines. The fact that I am writing the diary at a time when I am so busy is probably what gives it value.[4]

Takami is known chiefly as a novelist, though he wrote poetry and nonfiction, as well as the diary. The diary brought him neither fame nor money, but he never seriously considered abandoning it, time-consuming though it was. Sometimes he debated with himself whether to publish the diary. At first, he refused to think of publication, but later, he rewrote the diary of the war years and published the revised account in 1959 as *Haisen nikki* (*Diary of the Defeat*). The first eight volumes of the diary proper, covering 1941 to 1951, did not appear until 1965, the year of his death. This was followed by a posthumously published sequel, also in eight volumes.

The chief interest of Takami's diary is that he not only described what he saw or heard but invariably added comments. The harsh judgments he passed on individuals or on the Japanese people as a whole may have made him hesitate to publish the diary as it stood. His comments were generally acerbic, even when recounting some trivial occurrence. In November 1945, the Senbai Kōsha (Monopoly Corporation) staged a contest for the name of a new brand of cigarettes. The winning name was Peace. Takami wrote,

> During the war, English was totally forbidden. Cigarettes with long-familiar names like "Bat" and "Cherry" disappeared. But

now English names have been given a new lease on life, thanks to our having been defeated by English-speaking countries. One might suppose a Japanese name would have done just as well, but we go from one extreme to the other. The superficiality of the Japanese can be glimpsed even in such things. "Corona" wouldn't be bad, but isn't "Peace" a bit demeaning? It's like something out of a comic novel. A bellicose country loses a war and the next instant raises the cry of "Peace! Peace!"[5]

Sometimes the implications of an experience make Takami's tone despondent. On October 24, passing by a movie theater with a friend, he suddenly felt like going in. In the past, he had regularly attended films, at least once a week, but it had been such a long time since he last saw one that he had almost forgotten what they were like. This one was called *Soyokaze* (*Breezes*). He asked his friend about the movie and was told, "I hear it's terrible. Japanese films have gone to pot." Takami went into the theater anyway, curious to see what made the movie so terrible. *Sayokaze*, the first postwar film, was famous for its "Apple Song," which became extraordinarily popular.[6] There was standing room only in the theater. Takami, however, was by no means impressed:

It was absolutely appalling. It was the story of how three musicians who work in a revue theater, detecting musical talent in the young woman who does the lighting, decide to train her to be a star. The story is stupid, and the film techniques could not have been more idiotic. I wondered when Japanese films became so crude.

I recalled seeing in Southeast Asia the inane musical films of the natives. I felt they provided plain evidence of the shallowness of culture in the colonies. It was not so much contempt as oppressive grief that assailed me. I felt so strongly on this subject because these people belong to the same yellow race.

What would Occupation soldiers feel if they saw this ugly, superficial, utterly frivolous, shameful Japanese copy of an American musical? . . .

"Are you still so vain?" I asked myself. "Even after you've seen every day with your own eyes how things are at present—Japanese wandering through the streets like beggars, soliciting money from American soldiers? Even though Japanese culture is in the same abysmal state as that Japanese film? This is the plain truth, but are you still trying to avert your eyes? It's not the vulgar Japanese film that you should feel ashamed of, but your own vanity that makes you think the film is vulgar." This is what I told myself, but the sadness did not leave me. My heart has been wounded, and the wound has not easily healed.[7]

Takami, having written these lines, summed up his grief in a poem that opens

Every day my heart receives a wound.
I am covered with wounds, covered with blood.
Covered with wounds, I do not think of escaping, I do not try to
escape.
I will accept my fill of wounds.

Takami did not intend this poem to be read by others; he had no wish to proclaim his sensitivity, nor did he want to play the role of the tormented intellectual. His writings before the war had conveyed not only political concerns but a love for the tawdry world of Asakusa, with its bars and brothels. Little in Takami's manner suggested that he would ever write of his wounds. But every day in the new Japan, though he longer feared the police, he received a fresh wound.

During the war, Takami had felt a deep awareness of being Japanese. When he saw a line of Japanese patiently waiting to buy train tickets, he felt that he wanted to live and die with these humble people.[8] He had written that he was ready to die for his country. After the war, however, Takami tended to lose this solidarity with his compatriots, and he penned intemperate criticism of Japan and the Japanese. The vulgarity of *Soyokaze* not only irritated him but made him liken the Japanese to the colonized peoples of Southeast Asia. Almost any event related in his postwar diary is likely to end with the revelation of some unattractive or even contemptible truth he has discovered about the Japanese.

Immediately following his reactions to *Sayokaze*, Takami related the story of a younger brother of the noted psychoanalyst Shikiba Ryūzaburō who had been drafted and sent to Saipan. It was assumed that he had been killed in the *gyokusai* that ended Japanese resistance on the island. One day, an American officer visited Shikiba with a letter that, he said, the brother had asked him to deliver. Shikiba, sure that his brother had died a year earlier, told the American that he must be mistaken, but the American insisted that he had seen Shikiba's brother the previous week and produced the letter.

Shikiba learned from the letter that his brother had been taken prisoner by the American army. The purpose in writing was to ask what treatment he could expect as a former prisoner in the event that he returned to Japan. If, as was true in the past, he would be executed, he would remain in Saipan and somehow make a living.[9]

Takami did not say what happened to Shikiba's brother. Instead, he described the contempt and animosity shown by Japanese who became prisoners after the war toward those who had become prisoners during the war. This example of the hatred of Japanese for other Japanese, stemming from the belief that a soldier who allowed himself to become a prisoner of war deserved death, saddened Takami. It also made him aware that, without realizing it, he had come to adopt the American attitude that being taken prisoner was not a disgrace. He had been indoctrinated to believe that it was natural to put a prisoner to death, but this conviction now seemed unnatural. Takami considered the traditional attitude toward prisoners proof of the inhumanity of Japanese society.

Takami's diary shifts at this point to an account of changing trains at Ōfuna the same day, October 24. A young Japanese woman whom he had seen walking on the platform with an American soldier boarded the train. The soldier remained behind. The woman stuck her head out of the window to chat with him. Presently, the train began to move, and she called out, "*Baibai.*" All the passengers in the car had by now turned toward the woman, their expressions showing contempt and even hatred. Takami continues,

I was one of them. I wanted to see the expression on the woman's face. She continued to lean from the window. She looked as if she intended never to leave it. Her stance showed she was fully aware of the gaze of the other passengers and the emotions in their eyes. It also revealed that awareness of what was in their eyes aroused neither her resistance nor her enmity.

I gradually began to sense the pathos of the scene. She had come to look like a woman at a so-called "special comfort facility." Before long, this girl, who was not a professional, might actually feel proud to behave shockingly with an American soldier even when surrounded by watching eyes. Such sights might, unexpectedly soon, cease to seem unusual.

It would actually be a good thing if that happened very soon. Best of all would be a deluge of such sights. It would be good training for the Japanese!

Afterward, natural, not shameful, beautiful social relations will come into being.[10]

Takami's conclusion was highly unusual. For most Japanese men (including Takami a short while earlier), the sight of a Japanese woman behaving immodestly with an American soldier was the least welcome feature of the Occupation. But Takami, refusing to submit to the prejudices of Japanese society, saw in such couples the beginnings of relations without racial discrimination. Perhaps he mentally contrasted American soldiers strolling with Japanese women on a street or station platform with Japanese soldiers waiting their turn outside a Chinese brothel.

Often in his diary, Takami wrote of initially sharing the prejudices of other Japanese, only suddenly to realize that such attitudes were mistaken. A month after seeing the woman on the train, Takami attended an exhibition of ukiyo-e. A cabaret was housed on another floor of the same building. Outside the cabaret was the sign "Allied Armed Forces Only." It reminded Takami of signs in Shanghai parks that read "Chinese and Dogs Keep Out." Now, on the Ginza, a sign said, in effect, "Japanese Keep Out." Takami was at first shocked, but quickly changed his mind:

It can't be helped, considering that we are under an occupying power. But it is worth noting that the sign refusing admission to Japanese was put up by Japanese, and the cabaret that Japanese were not allowed to enter was built by Japanese. It is also noteworthy that this enterprise is under the management of a right-wing organization that, before the war ended, called for "respect for the emperor and expulsion of the barbarians."

I wonder if one could find a similar example elsewhere in the world. People of an occupied country who can't wait to assemble women and build brothels for an occupying army. Not in China. Nor in Southeast Asia. Even the Chinese, who are skilled at appeasing their enemies, never rounded up Chinese women, turned them into prostitutes, and established a market in human flesh for the occupying Japanese army. The Chinese never did anything so shameful. Is it not true that only the Japanese could do such a thing?

The Japanese army always took prostitutes with them to the front. Many prostitutes were Korean, allegedly because Korean women had strong bodies. Almost all of them were tricked into being chosen. Japanese women were also tricked and carried off to Southeast Asia. They were told they would be clerks in canteens, then loaded aboard ships. When they reached the assigned locations, they were informed with threats that they were to work at comfort stations. I hear that some women committed suicide. Those unable to kill themselves became in tears prostitutes. Such cruelty was carried out in the name of winning the war.[11]

For all his criticism, Takami did not lose his love for his country. On March 6, 1946, he went to see *Madame Curie*, the first American film he had seen in years. It was preceded by an American newsreel:

It showed Special Attack Force planes crashing into American warships. Everybody applauded. With tears in my eyes, I also applauded.

I detest the military clique. But I cannot detest Japan. I cannot discard my love for my country. I grieve from the heart for the dead heroes of the Special Attack Force.

This feeling took the form of applause. The applause of the others in the theater was probably an expression of the same feelings.

If an American had been present in the theater and heard the applause, he might have thought, "The Japanese still haven't lost their enmity."

But the applause was not an expression of enmity, though perhaps the propagandistic American newsreel in fact stirred up enmity among some Japanese. This kind of propaganda film, which portrays America as the only righteous country and America's enemies as merciless enemies of justice, may actually stir up enmity that would have melted away naturally if left alone or that perhaps from the start had never existed.[12]

Yamada Fūtarō saw *Madame Curie* on June 18. He commented,

Madame Curie did not live up to its reputation. It is not a wholly successful film, but the scene where, at the very moment the husband and wife discover radium, the lovable Dr. Curie is run over and killed by a horse carriage and his wife grieves for him could not fail to excite the tears of the audience. The film is not as good as *Watch on the Rhine* but better than *Keys of the Kingdom*. Not one of all the American films in the recent flood of importations has been as good as the French films, but it is regrettably true that they are a degree superior to Japanese films.

Yamada was irritated by the newsreel accompanying the feature film, which ostentatiously displayed American military might. There were also scenes of German war criminals being executed, some by a firing squad and others by hanging. The audience watched on silently, stunned, as American bullets struck blindfolded men, who crumpled to the ground. Yamada commented, "Ah, how detestable is the uncompromising nature of the white men! Would they have been able to invent the atomic bomb if it had not been in their nature to make such films and display them publicly?"[13]

Takami regretted that blatant American propaganda films might harm relations with the Japanese; Yamada seemed pleased to have found in the newsreel additional reasons to hate the Americans. He declared that the most important cause of the war was the cry that had filled New York when the war broke out—"Little Japs! The gall of them!" Now that Japan had been defeated, the Americans would have all the more reason to look down on the Japanese. He had been profoundly disappointed when the emperor announced his acceptance of the Allied demand for unconditional surrender, but he believed that the strength of young Japanese would make it possible to defeat the Americans in the next war and smash their superiority complex:

> At the very least, we will create a situation that will make them treat the Japanese as equals. —The only means of achieving this is a Japanese victory. —At the appropriate time, we must make plans to take revenge on America. This may be forever impossible, but it is even more impossible to permit America to consider Japan eternally as a fourth-rate nation. . . . —The cause and effect of endless war . . . but this is unavoidable. We prefer to struggle in a perpetual sea of blood rather than be looked upon as inferiors, to be slaves.[14]

Yamada had not been conscripted for military service. He never took part in fighting, though his medical school and lodgings were bombed, and he witnessed the destruction of Tokyo. It may have been easier for him than for a man who had actually experienced warfare to advocate plunging the country into "a perpetual sea of blood." He also wrote that Japan had started the "holy war" in order to liberate the countries of Asia from white colonial rule.[15] This ideal came later, as we have seen, but when the liberation of Asia was proclaimed as Japan's war aim, many Japanese readily adopted the notion that Japan was fighting to free people of the same color as themselves.

There was, however, a snag in the claim that Japan had fought a war of liberation. The long conflict with China could not easily be explained as part of such a struggle. Yamada had a response: Chiang Kai-shek, for all his boasts, was unable to free Manchuria completely from the Soviet menace. Were not Soviet troops now stationed in Manchuria? Only Japan could ensure that Manchuria would be wholly and eternally in Asian hands. He admitted that Japan had made a mistake in starting the Pacific War too soon, before its scientific knowledge had sufficiently matured and before its people had been sufficiently educated for the task. Addressing the peoples of Asia, he wrote in his diary, "Because Japan's strength was inadequate, our good intentions, despite ourselves, brought you painful tragedy. We apologize. But wait for tomorrow. Wait for the day when we compel the white men, who have too long treated Asia with contempt, to make a truly human self-examination."[16]

The Occupation, carried out by the Americans and their allies, brought a large number of white men to Japan in the role of conquerors. This boded ill for relations between the races, but contrary to expectations, the Occupation on the whole went well and resulted in an establishment of friendship rather than an increase of enmity. Ironically, the defeat brought Japan the recognition that Yamada supposed could come only with victory in war. The Japanese language, previously taught hardly anywhere outside the Japanese Empire, came to be studied at universities in all advanced countries, along with the history and literature of Japan. The Japanese economy was praised as a marvel to be emulated, and Western businessmen read Miyamoto Musashi's *Gorin no sho* (*Book of the Rings*, ca. 1645) for guidance. Japanese merchandise was sought abroad not because it was cheap (the reason before the war) but because it was high-quality. Possibly more Western people were attracted to Zen than Japanese were drawn to Christianity. One wonders if so much prestige would have accrued to Japan if Japan had been victorious.

Vengeance is a recurrent theme in Yamada's diary of the Occupation. On August 3, 1946, large formations of B-29s flew over Tokyo in a display of peacetime power. According to Yamada, there was not one smiling Japanese face among those who observed the planes. He quoted a policeman's wife who told her young son, "Japan used to have airplanes, but we got beaten in the war and there aren't any left. Not even one. When you become a big boy, we'll have another war, and we'll win and you'll ride in an airplane." Yamada commented, "The Americans say that the Japanese have no sense of humor. But what's so funny about flying over cities you've bombed indiscriminately and intimidating them? The Japanese will not smile again until the day of vengeance."[17]

The diary entry for August 15 is labeled "Vengeance Memorial Day."[18] On September 25, Yamada declared, "No matter how much the newspapers praise America, there lies dormant in ninety percent of the youth of Japan the resolve to take up bravely the sword of vengeance as soon as a spark is struck."[19]

Perhaps Yamada really believed that 90 percent of the youth were itching to avenge the defeat, but he could not ignore the satisfaction with peace felt by the average Japanese. He wrote on October 22:

There flows deep within the hearts of present-day Japanese the selfish, pitiful, comic mistake of thinking "Now that the war has ended, we ought to be able to live somewhat more comfortably." The war didn't end of itself. We were beaten. It's not as if a storm wind for which we were not responsible had suddenly stopped blowing. Thinking of the war in such terms has led only to stupid dissatisfaction, which in turn has developed into a feeling of resignation to the Will of Heaven and Fate. Resignation may be bliss, but if the peoples of East Asia stay resigned, they will be unable, even after ten thousand years have elapsed, to escape their condition as slaves. We were beaten. By whom? By our enemies! America, England, Russia![20]

On November 30, Yamada wrote,

Only the newspapers, in their fickle way, rejoice in democracy or whatever it's called. In the breasts of the entire Japanese people there is a feeling of grave despair imprinted with something like lead. Wherever one may go, no matter from whose breast one might peel the skin, one will find the desire to rise again and for vengeance—that and nothing else.[21]

Yamada detested not only the Americans but the Soviet Russians, and he seldom missed an opportunity to abuse both. He was no more favorably disposed toward the British, the oppressors of India, though he praised Australian soldiers who, unlike the Americans, did not chew gum. He admired French films and read very widely in French literature, ranging from the plays of Victor Hugo and Alfred de Musset to the works of Paul Valéry, but accused the French of having subdued the Vietnamese with gunfire.[22]

The only country he admired without qualification was Japan. He read a great deal of French and Russian literature but almost as much Japanese literature, history, and philosophy. Most often, he made no comment on the books he read. He did not state, for example, what attracted him to the writings of Nakae Tōju (1609–1648), the founder in Japan of the Wang Yangming school of Confucianism, though we may infer that it was the emphasis this school gave to the importance of implementing thought with action.

Yamada read incessantly. He was especially fond of Nagai Kafū. On reading Kafū's short story "Odoriko" (The Dancer), he wrote, "It has been quite some time since I read such a story. I read it voraciously. I even thought that I would not regret our having lost the war if that was what made it possible for me to read this story. In its subtlety, charm and pathos his art is closer to poetry than to fiction and rises to ever more absolute realms."[23]

Yamada knew that Kafū's books had been banned during the war and that many people had consequently forgotten him, but despite his admiration for Kafū, he concluded that his works had represented a danger to the state and that it was therefore proper for the government to have suppressed them. Reading a story by Kafū about the love affair between a musician and a dancer in Asakusa brought the reader ten thousand times more pleasure than did a stupid war story, but a war story, however clumsy, would never arouse deeply antiwar sentiments.

However, there was a real danger that descriptions of the pleasures formerly enjoyed in Asakusa might be so seductive to ordinary readers as to make them hate the war. The government could not have permitted such sentiments to arise.

Many authors, unlike Kafū, had continued to publish during the war. After the defeat, some claimed that, though they actually had opposed the war, they had been forced to comply with government directives. This was not untrue, but Yamada questioned such men's commitment to freedom. He declared that if the Americans and British were to withdraw from Japan, the Japanese would not know how to manage freedom of speech or any other kind of freedom:[24]

> The Japanese have definitely not acquired either freedom or peace. Objective facts dispassionately reveal that the path Japan is now pursuing leads to a dark, cold graveyard. Unless a time comes when Japanese realize this clearly and thoroughly, Japan will never rise again. Freedom and peace must be seized with one's own hands. They are certainly not something that can be bestowed by others and enjoyed afterward.[25]

Yamada wrote mockingly of those who rejoiced in the new freedom and thanked General MacArthur for having freed the Japanese people from the yoke of the military clique. The only freedom for which Yamada was grateful was being able to read the works of Nagai Kafū.

Freedom is mentioned from time to time in his diary, but never as a sought-for ideal. It is puzzling, considering his readings, that Yamada should not have felt the importance of freedom. But though his derogation of freedom and his cries for revenge continued into the postwar period, another theme emerged in his diary. He had discovered his métier as a writer, and this would be his salvation.

Even as a middle-school student, Yamada had submitted stories to magazines that were accepted for publication. He seems not to have written anything during the war years apart from the diary, but he mentioned from time to time in 1946 that he was working on a story. On March 6, he wrote the outline of a story called "Fukushū" (Vengeance), which, surprisingly, is not concerned with the United States.[26] On July 12, he asked himself, "Shall I try to write a *Comédie humaine*? I'll add to the *Comédie humaine* the *Rougon-Macquart*. It will be set in the Meiji, Taishō, and Shōwa eras, the time of the greatest glory and shame of all Japanese history."[27]

On July 15, he mentioned that he had completed the plan for two stories: "The Incident at Daruma Pass" and "The Demon in Sight." The former won the prize of the mystery magazine *Hōseki* and was published in the January 1947 issue, marking the beginning of Yamada's career as a writer of mysteries and stories about ninja. But he had higher ambitions, as he wrote on December 22, 1946:

> Mystery stories are no more than a hobby. I have not the slightest intention of writing mystery stories for the rest of my life. I have plans for a great many historical novels, works of science fiction, satires, modern novels. But now we are in the midst of a paper shortage, not a propitious moment for new writers to make their début. One can count on the fingers of both hands the active writers of mysteries. . . . All I hope for is, by using my medical knowledge, to be recognized as the eleventh.[28]

Yamada also hoped to become a newspaper reporter. The income would relieve the burden on the uncle who supported him, but his aim was not merely financial:

> Japan stands before the abyss of national ruin. In order to save it from ruin, I would like to attack mercilessly and make tremble with fear the corrupt officials and profiteers who, together with deceitful Chinese and Korean merchants, exploit a people gasping in misery. It will not deter me even if, as a result, my life is put in danger. But in order accomplish this, I must acquire a knowledge of politics and economics. —The main enemy is America.[29]

Yamada, contrary to his hopes, did not become a crusading journalist, but he certainly became, at the very least, the eleventh most distinguished writer of mystery stories, and he published many other works, including some based on Chinese and Japanese history. It is not clear when, if ever, he abandoned his intention of taking vengeance against the United States.[30]

Takami Jun's postwar writings, leaving behind the world of Asakusa, dealt with such issues as the problem of freedom.[31] He could now reveal that he had not lost the Marxist convictions he had disavowed before the police fifteen years earlier, but he refused to allow doctrine to take the place of literary value. His most impressive novel, *Iya na kanji* (*Feelings of Disgust*), published in 1963, is concerned with anarchism, a revolutionary movement whose central aim was freedom. With respect to freedom, Takami and Yamada were many miles apart.

The postwar world was richer for the writings of such contrasting figures as Takami Jun and Yamada Fūtarō, though they may be remembered in the future less for the novels that brought them fame than for the diaries in which they recorded what it meant to be a Japanese at a time of disaster and transformation. Many other authors would later set down recollections of wartime experiences, but one cannot be sure that they are free from hindsight or from an author's natural tendency to impose structure and polish on events that were in fact much less literary. Diaries are more likely to approximate the truth.

Introduction

1. Samuel Hideo Yamashita translated eleven wartime diaries by people of widely different professions and ages in *Leaves from an Autumn of Emergencies*. Etsuko Ohnuki-Tierney published translations of excerpts from the diaries of kamikaze pilots in *Kamikaze Diaries*.

2. European authors whom Yamada read before August 15, 1945, included Chekhov (many works), Balzac (many works), Gorky, Gogol, Schnitzler, Maeterlinck (many works), Jules Renard, Tolstoy, Stendhal, August de Villiers de L'Isle-Adam, Gide, Pierre Loti, Gabriele D'Annunzio, Henri de Régnier, George Gissing, and Flaubert. After August 15, he read Engels, Hans Carrossa, Ibsen, Zola, Dickens, Paul Bourget, and various works of Japanese literature. His favorite author, judging from the number of works he read, was Balzac. He does

not specify whether he read the European works in the original languages or in Japanese translation, but I imagine he read French and German authors in the originals.

3. Entry for January 31, 1944, in Yamada Fūtarō, *Senchūha fusen nikki*, p. 56.

4. Entry for September 29, 1943, in Kiyosawa Kiyoshi, *Ankoku nikki*, p. 95, and *A Diary of Darkness*, p. 87.

5. Entry for June 22, 1944, in Kiyosawa, *Ankoku nikki*, p. 192, and *Diary of Darkness*, p. 207.

6. Entry for June 28, 1944, in Kiyosawa, *Ankoku nikki*, p. 195, and *Diary of Darkness*, p. 210.

7. Entry for August 20, 1944, in Kiyosawa, *Ankoku nikki*, p. 222, and *Diary of Darkness*, p. 244.

8. Entry for January 1, 1945, in Kiyosawa, *Ankoku nikki*, p. 262, and *Diary of Darkness*, p. 299.

9. Entry for August 15, 1945, in Tokugawa Musei, *Musei sensō nikki shō*, pp. 89–90.

10. The wartime diary of Kiyosawa Kiyoshi, *Ankoku nikki*, was translated in its entirety by Eugene Soviak and Kamiyama Tamie as *A Diary of Darkness*.

Nagai Kafū's diary was used, notably, by Edward Seidensticker in *Kafū the Scribbler*. In making my translations from Kafū's diary, I have used *Nagai Kafū nikki*, published in 1959 by Tōto Shoten. The version of the diary found in *Kafū zenshū*, published in 1963 by Iwanami Shoten, is close to the Tōto Shoten text, but there are numerous minor changes, often simplifying Kafū's highly literary expression. The diary called *Risai nichiroku*, the first version to be published (in 1947), is quite different from the other two and may be a rewriting. But the order of the three versions has not been established. Ōno Shigeo, in *Kafū nikki kenkyū* (pp. 308–73), gives parallel passages dating from 1917 to 1948 from the two main lines of text. Nagai Hisamitsu, Kafū's adopted son, mentioned in *Chichi Nagai Kafū* (pp. 26, 91) that two men were employed by Kafū during the war to make copies of the diary. These copies, which had disappeared by the time Hisamitsu moved into Kafū's house in Ichikawa, may have been the source of the textual variants.

The diaries of Takami Jun, Itō Sei, and Yamada Fūtarō—my principal "informants"—have not, as far as I know, been examined in detail by scholars in Japan or elsewhere.

1. The Day the War Began

1. Because Japan is on the other side of the International Date Line from Hawaii, from the Japanese point of view, the attack on Pearl Harbor occurred on December 8 rather than on December 7, 1941.

2. Entry for January 1, 1942, in *Aono Suekichi nikki*, p. 129.

3. Entry for December 8, 1941, in *Nagai Kafū nikki*, vol. 6, p. 76.

4. Entry for December 12, 1941, in ibid. Kafū is mocking wartime slogans that, in the attempt to make them powerful, end with the copula *da*, a blunt colloquial form. The last sentence puns on the sound *da*, which here means "inept" or "no good."

5. Takamura Kōtarō, "Jūnigatsu yōka," in *Takamura Kōtarō zenshū*, vol. 3, p. 3.

6. Some sources say that Leonie Gilmour was his common-law wife (she referred to herself as Mrs. Noguchi); others claim that he never recognized her as his wife. For an account of their complicated relationship, see Masayo Duus, *The Life of Isamu Noguchi*. The child of their union was the celebrated sculptor Isamu Noguchi.

7. Noguchi Yonejirō, "Slaughter Them!" in *Hakkōshō ippyakuhen*, pp. 119–21.

8. Quoted in Odagiri Susumu, "Zoku jūnigatsu yōka no kiroku," p. 107.

9. Entry for December 8, 1941, in Itō Sei, *Taiheiyō Sensō nikki*, vol. 1, p. 11.

10. Itō Sei, "Kono kandō naezaran ga tame ni," in *Itō Sei zenshū*, vol. 15, pp. 162–67.

11. An interesting discussion of what the term *minzoku* meant to the Japanese is given by Tessa Morris-Suzuki: "Like *Volk*, *minzoku* has powerful overtones of communal solidarity, but is equivocal about the basis of the solidarity. While race is clearly based on inherited physical characteristics, a minzoku may be held together by blood bonds, nationality, culture or some combination of these things" ("Descent into the Past," p. 88). She also quoted Kita Sadakichi to the effect that *minzoku* was not a matter of biology but of culture and, above all, of ideology (p. 89).

12. Entry for December 16, 1941, in Itō, *Taiheiyō Sensō nikki*, vol. 1, p. 21.

13. Entry for December 12, 1941, in ibid., p. 20.

14. Entry for March 3, 1942, in ibid., p. 70.

15. Entry for March 12, 1942, in ibid., p. 74.

16. Yoshida Ken'ichi, "Henshū kōki," *Hihyō*, January 1, 1942.

17. Quoted in Yoneda Toshiaki, "Ichi gunkoku shugisha to tanka," p. 55.

18. Entry for January 7, 1945, in *Takami Jun nikki*, vol. 3, p. 9.

19. Entry for August 1, 1943, in Kiyosawa Kiyoshi, *Ankoku nikki*, p. 71, and *A Diary of Darkness*, p. 60. The publisher was Shimanaka Yūsaku, the president of Chūō kōron sha.

20. Entry for December 17, 1944, in Itō, *Taiheiyō Sensō nikki*, vol. 3, p. 199.

21. Yamada later became a writer of popular fiction, known especially for his accounts of *ninja*. At this time, he was studying to become an army doctor.

22. Entry for January 1, 1945, in Yamada Fūtarō, *Senchūha fusen nikki*, p. 11.

23. Entry for April 19, 1942, in Itō, *Taiheiyō Sensō nikki*, vol. 1, pp. 108–9.

24. Entries for April 18 and 19, 1942, in *Nagai Kafū nikki*, vol. 6, pp. 95–96.

25. Matsuura Sōzō, *Senjika no genron tōsei*, pp. 62–64.

26. Entry for January 16, 1945, in *Nagai Kafū nikki*, vol. 7, p. 9.
27. Minami Hiroshi, "Ryūgen higo ni arawareta minshū no teikō ishiki," pp. 1–3.
28. Entry for January 6, 1945, in Yamada, *Senchūha fusen nikki*, p. 17. A name like *Pōsuke* may have been a farcical corruption of Boeing.
29. *Unno Jūza haisen nikki*, p. 11.
30. Entry for January 6, 1945, in Yamada, *Senchūha fusen nikki*, p. 23.
31. Ibid., p. 14.
32. Entry for January 3, 1945, in ibid., p. 12.
33. Entry for January 1, 1945, in Kiyosawa, *Ankoku nikki*, p. 261, and *Diary of Darkness*, p. 298.
34. Entry for January 2, 1945, in Kiyosawa, *Ankoku nikki*, p. 263, and *Diary of Darkness*, p. 300.

2. The Birth of "Greater East Asia"

1. Kiyosawa Kiyoshi could think of only two prominent men who opposed the war: Ishibashi Tanzan (1884–1973) and Baba Tsunego (1865–1956). Entry for April 3, 1945, in Kiyosawa, *Ankoku nikki*, p. 165, and *A Diary of Darkness*, p. 170. For an account of the joyous reaction of writers to the outbreak of war, see Sakuramoto Tomio, *Nihon Bungaku Hōkokukai*, pp. 56–70.
2. Entry for November 19, 1943, in Itō Sei, *Taiheiyō Sensō nikki*, vol. 2, p. 188.
3. When Emperor Meiji learned of the Japanese victory at Port Arthur during the Russo-Japanese War, his first reaction was not one of joy but of admiration for General Anatoly Stössel's unwavering loyalty to his country. He ordered Yamagata Aritomo to make sure that Stössel was allowed to maintain his dignity.
4. Quoted in Kiyosawa, *Ankoku nikki*, p. 146, and *Diary of Darkness*, p. 147. Kiyosawa wrote that the Japanese treated prisoners of war as if they were criminals. It was considered quite normal to administer severe physical punishment to criminals, and prisoners therefore were also beaten.
5. The American victory at Midway in June 1942 is more commonly cited as the "turning point," but as yet the Imperial Japanese Army had suffered no setbacks.
6. Entry for December 5, 1942, in Itō, *Taiheiyō Sensō nikki*, vol. 1, pp. 219–20.
7. Itō had been born and raised in Hokkaidō.
8. In 1939, the village of Nomonhan on the border between Mongolia and Manchukuo had been the scene of a battle between the Japanese and Soviet armies. The Japanese were defeated.
9. Entry for May 31, 1943, in Itō, *Taiheiyō Sensō nikki*, vol. 1, pp. 341–44.
10. Entry for June 5, 1943, in ibid., p. 349.
11. Entry for May 31, 1943, in *Takami Jun nikki*, vol. 2b, p. 559.

12. Maekawa Samio, in *Sensō bungaku zenshū*, ed. Hirano Ken, *bessatsu*, pp. 208–9. It originally appeared in the collection *Kongō*.

13. *The Complete Poetry and Prose of Chairil Anwar*, pp. 168–69. "Jamasaki" is the Dutch or Indonesian spelling of "Yamasaki."

14. Kusunoki Masashige (d. 1336) was a warrior described in prewar school textbooks as a model of loyalty to the imperial house.

15. Entry for June 1, 1943, in *Nagai Kafū nikki*, vol. 6, pp. 157–58.

16. Entry for June 3, 1943, in ibid., p. 158. The terms *sakoku* (closure of the country) and *jōi* (expulsion of barbarians) were used by nationalist patriots as slogans at the end of the Tokugawa period. Kafū is likening those days to his own.

17. Attu enjoys only some eight to ten days of sunshine in an entire year.

18. Teigeki is a shortened version of Teikoku Gekijō, or Imperial Theater. It first opened in 1911, but was severely damaged in the Great Kantō Earthquake of 1923 and was rebuilt.

19. Yoshida Ken'ichi, "Henshū kōki," *Hihyō*, December 1942.

20. The slogan *hakkō ichiu*, often employed during the war years, predicted the harmonious unity of the entire world once it came under Japanese rule. Its origin has been traced back to the *Nihon shoki* (*Chronicles of Japan*, 720), but, as used during the war, was the creation (in 1903) of the Buddhist priest Tanaka Chigaku (1861–1939).

21. Ozaki Hotsuki, "Daitōa bungakusha taikai ni tsuite," p. 22.

22. The Japanese had granted independence to Burma on August 1, 1943, and the Philippines were declared independent on October 14, 1943.

23. For an account of this ruling, found in the Daitōa Seiryaku Shidō Taikō, see Miwa Kimitada, *Nihon*, p. 174. The decision to give these countries independence was not made until after Hiroshima and Nagasaki had been destroyed by atomic bombs.

24. Fukada Yūsuke, *Reimei no seiki*, p. 8. According to Ba Maw, "India was outside the Japanese concept of Greater East Asia" (*Breakthrough in Burma*, p. 355).

25. Ba Maw, *Breakthrough in Burma*, p. 337.

26. Fukada, *Reimei no seiki*, p. 25.

27. Ibid., pp. 77–83.

28. Miwa, *Nihon*, p. 171; Fukada, *Reimei no seiki*, pp. 82–83. A photograph taken in 1943, included in the section "Speeches, Messages & Statements," shows Laurel distributing "foodstuffs to families of men picked up by the Japanese soldiers and who never returned to their homes" (*José P. Laurel*, p. 22).

29. *José P. Laurel*, p. 24.

30. Ibid., p. 272.

31. Ba Maw wrote, "There cannot be the slightest doubt that the hard-core, fire-eating militarists within the Japanese army behaved brutally.... Their early

dazzling victories turned the heads of many of them. They brought out the evil, predatory side of the Japanese character" (*Breakthrough in Burma*, p. 180).

32. Fukada, *Reimei no seiki*, pp. 81–83. See also Ba Maw, *Breakthrough in Burma*, pp. 176–92.

33. Ba Maw, *Breakthrough in Burma*, p. 343.

34. Quoted in ibid., p. 285. The article from which this is extracted appeared in *Burma*, the organ of wartime Foreign Affairs Association. I have not seen this journal.

35. Jorge B. Vargas, in *World War II and the Japanese Occupation*, ed. Ricardo Trota Jose, p. 129. Vargas became the wartime Filipino ambassador to Japan. Shortly before the Japanese troops were driven from Manila, he was quoted as asserting, "We know Japan is destined for sure victory and prosperity for ages to come."

Jose quotes other leaders like Benigno Aquino, who insisted that the Filipinos were Asians and rejoiced in Japan's "magnificent doctrine of the Co-Prosperity Sphere" (p. 130). Other leaders refused to cooperate with the Japanese, and Laurel, despite his policy of friendship with the Japanese, was extremely reluctant to agree when the Japanese demanded that the Philippines declare war on the United States (p. 156).

36. Fukada, *Reimei no seiki*, p. 120.

37. For an account of these organizations, giving the names of the principal members, see Sakuramoto, *Nihon Bungaku Hōkokukai*, pp. 21–76.

38. Entry for February 13, 1947, in *Nagai Kafū nikki*, vol. 6, p. 155.

39. Uchida Hyakken, *Tōkyō shōjin*, pp. 149–50.

40. Entry of July 22, 1945, in *Takami Jun nikki*, vol. 4, p. 273.

41. Inoue Shirō, *Shōgen, senji bundanshi*, pp. 10–14; *Hirano Ken zenshū*, vol. 13, p. 385. Sugino Yōkichi's *Aru hihyōka no shōzō* is a six hundred–page book on Hirano's wartime activities.

42. For a detailed list of the accomplishments of the Bunpō, including the names of participants, see Sakuramoto, *Nihon Bungaku Hōkokukai*, pp. 139–360.

3. False Victories and Real Defeats

1. Entry for November 30, 1943, in Itō Sei, *Taiheiyō Sensō nikki*, vol. 2, p. 205.

2. Ibid., pp. 203–4.

3. Entry for July 2, 1943, in ibid., p. 8.

4. I have not found any statement by Grew of this nature. Grew, known for his sympathy for the Japanese, opposed dropping the atomic bomb.

5. Entry for July 14, 1943, in Itō, *Taiheiyō Sensō nikki*, vol. 2, p. 21.

6. Entry for August 13, 1943, in ibid., p. 49. Itō was quoting a dispatch from Buenos Aires that appeared in the *Yomiuri shinbun*. The remark was attributed to one Kilfler (? Ki-ru-fu-ra).

7. Entry for December 2, 1943, in ibid., p. 209.

8. Entry for March 10, 1944, in Kiyosawa Kiyoshi, *Ankoku nikki*, pp. 150–51, and *A Diary of Darkness*, p. 153.

9. Entry for July 27, 1943, in Itō, *Taiheiyō Sensō nikki*, vol. 2, p. 31.

10. Entry for August 30, 1943, in ibid, p. 65.

11. Entry for August 5, 1943, in ibid., p. 41.

12. Entry for November 10, 1943, in ibid., p. 172.

13. Entry for November 8, 1943, in ibid., p. 172; entry for July 20, 1944, in ibid., vol. 3, p. 65.

14. Saitō Mokichi, editorial, *Araragi*, December 1944.

15. Ishikawa Jun, *Bungaku taigai*, p. 139. Ishikawa expressed admiration for Thomas Mann's (supposed) refusal to speak ill of the Nazis even after leaving Germany.

16. Entry for December 15, 1943, in Kiyosawa, *Ankoku nikki*, p. 119, and *Diary of Darkness*, p. 120.

17. Entry for July 1944, in Itō, *Taiheiyō Sensō nikki*, vol. 3, p. 61.

18. In the series of articles "Chichi Itō Sei no Nikki wo yomu," Itō Rei, the second son of Itō Sei, described his father's diary almost entirely in terms of his qualities as a father and as a friend. Rei did not mention Itō's consuming interest in the mission of the Yamato race.

19. Entries for September 22, 1943; October 16, 1943; November 25, 1943; and March 10, 1944, in Itō, *Taiheiyō Sensō nikki*, vol. 2, pp. 88, 129, 196, 304.

20. Entry for July 8, 1943, in ibid., p. 14. The entry gives the name of the magazine: *Yōnen jidai*.

21. Entry for November 19, 1943, in ibid., p. 189. Okumura Kiwao, the assistant director of the Cabinet Information Bureau, in his introductory remarks given at the opening ceremonies of the Bunpō on May 3, 1942, described the ways in which literature must cooperate with the war effort. See his *Sonnō jōi no kessen*, pp. 374–79.

22. Entry for September 4, 1943, in Itō, *Taiheiyō Sensō nikki*, vol. 2, p. 71.

23. Entry for July 14, 1944, in ibid., vol. 3, p. 59.

24. Entry for December 17, 1944, in ibid., p. 199.

25. Entry for November 9, 1943, in ibid., vol. 2, p. 169.

26. Entry for November 29, 1943, in ibid., p. 202.

27. Entry for March 10, 1944, in ibid., p. 306.

28. Entry for October 18, 1944, in ibid., vol. 3, p. 136.

29. Kelly indeed died courageously in an attack on a Japanese cruiser, but, contrary to what is commonly believed, he did not receive the Congressional Medal of Honor, but the Distinguished Service Cross.

30. Entry for October 20, 1943, in Itō, *Taiheiyō Sensō nikki*, vol. 3. p. 140.

31. Entry for October 29, 1943, in ibid., p. 144.

32. Both the Japanese army and navy had planes that carried out suicide attacks on American warships. The army planes were known as Special Attack Force; the navy planes, as Kamikaze (divine wind), alluding to the winds that had destroyed the Mongol ships that came to conquer Japan in the thirteenth century.

33. Yokomitsu Riichi, "Tokkōtai," in *Teihon Yokomitsu Riichi zenshū*, vol. 14, pp. 293–94. The essay was originally published in *Bungei*, March 1945.

34. Entry for January 18, 1945, in Itō, *Taiheiyō Sensō nikki*, vol. 3, pp. 230–31.

35. Entry for February 8, 1945, in ibid., p. 246.

36. The reason for the change, according to Inoue Shirō, the head of the Information Section of the Bunpō, was not Mushakōji's supposed illness but extreme pressure from Nagayo, who was desperately eager to be appointed as head of the delegation. Inoue and others in the Information Section resisted because Nagayo was much less famous than Mushakōji, but in the end he yielded. After the war, Nagayo wrote that a fascistic official in the Bunpō had forced him, despite his strong reluctance, to serve as head of the delegation. See Inoue Shirō, *Shōgen, sensō bundan shi*, pp. 82–87.

37. Entry for November 13, 1944, in *Takami Jun nikki*, vol. 2b, p. 853.

38. Ibid., pp. 854–55.

39. For a somewhat fictionalized account by Takami of this experience, see Keene, *Dawn to the West*, vol. 1, pp. 873–74. The original text is in *Takami Jun zenshū*, vol. 3, p. 476.

40. Yamada Fūtarō attended a special gala performance at the Kabuki-za in which the great Uzaemon performed, but the theater was half empty. See entry for January 11, 1945, in Yamada, *Senchūha fusen nikki*, p. 31. A week later, when he went to a movie theater, there were only some fifteen people in the audience. See entry for January 18, 1945, in ibid, p. 44.

41. Entry for January 10, 1945, in *Takami Jun nikki*, vol. 3, p. 20.

42. Ibid., p. 19.

43. Entry for April 24, 1944, in ibid., vol. 2, p. 397. Osaragi Jirō also reported the rumor, but added the detail that the rice with which one ate one's *rakkyō* must be red. He commented, "It's something that one might suppose could only have happened in the late Tokugawa or early Meiji eras" (*Osaragi Jirō haisen nikki*, p. 174).

44. Entry for February 27, 1945, in *Takami Jun nikki*, vol. 3, pp. 176–78.

45. Entry for July 27, 1945, in ibid., vol. 4, p. 304.

4. A Dismal New Year

1. Entry for December 31, 1944, in *Nagai Kafū nikki*, vol. 6, p. 262.

2. The name Henkikan might be translated as "Eccentricity House," a suitable name for Kafū's residence. But it might also have had the meaning of "painted

house" (*penkikan*), as opposed to an unpainted Japanese-style wooden house, according to Edward Seidensticker, *Kafū the Scribbler*, p. 99. Kafū had the house built in 1920 in the Azabu district, a fashionable part of the city.

3. Entry for March 9–10, 1945, in *Nagai Kafū nikki*, vol. 7, pp. 19–20.

4. Entry for March 10, 1945, in ibid., pp. 21–22.

5. I have often heard people opine that Kafū doctored his diaries after the war in order to make them more acceptable under the Occupation. But I believe that the complete diary, published in seven volumes in 1958 and 1959, is authentic, and this is the version I have used. At least two other versions of the diary exist. Kafū discovered after the war ended that he could sell the diary. He accordingly rewrote sections in 1946 and published them in the magazine *Shinsei*. The full account of the war years, discussed and partly translated by David C. Earhart in "Nagai Kafū's Wartime Diary," was given the title *Risai nichiroku* (*Account of the Calamity*) when it was published in 1947. I believe that this was the newest version in time of composition.

The complete diary, known as *Danchōtei nichijō*, covers not only the war years but the whole period between 1917 and 1959, the year of Kafū's death.

A third version of the diary was published in *Kafū zenshū* in 1963. It is close to the text in the 1958/1959 edition of the diary, but there are many small differences in the wording. The differences were probably made not to emphasize Kafū's dislike of the militarists or any other political matter but to make the text easier to read for general readers. Unusual kanji and expressions of Chinese origin were replaced with ordinary Japanese words.

An earlier (1948–1953) edition of the complete works had omitted certain passages in the diary, according to Seidensticker, *Kafū the Scribbler*, pp. 347–48. The *Zenshū* contained these passages, which proved to be "chitchat of a vaguely malicious nature about persons still living." There were also various drafts and clean copies of the diaries. He believed that fragmentary duplications of diary entries "strongly suggest that once something was in draft it was not altered significantly, and that not a great deal was added to a draft." He felt that the variant texts gave no reason for doubting Kafū's integrity with respect to changing diary entries. In other words, the text in the 1958/1959 edition of the diary can be trusted.

6. Entry for March 10, 1945, in Yamada Fūtarō, *Senchūha fusen nikki*, p. 102.

7. Ibid., p. 108.

8. Entry for May 7, 1945, in ibid., p. 204.

9. As far back as September 1944, Suzuki had visited the Swedish minister to Japan, Widar Bagge, in the hope that Swedish intercession, possibly involving the king, could end the war. The ultimately unsuccessful negotiations continued until well into the spring of 1945.

10. Entry for February 1, 1945, in Yamada, *Senchūha fusen nikki*, p. 57.

11. Entry for May 3, 1945, in ibid., p. 198.

12. Entry for May 5, 1945, in ibid., p. 199

13. Entry for May 6, 1945, in ibid., p. 202.

14. Entry for May 8, 1945, in ibid., p. 207.

15. Entry for June 4, 1945, in ibid., pp. 278–79.

16. Ibid., p. 279.

17. Entry for May 21, 1945, in ibid., p. 226.

18. Entry for May 23, 1945, in ibid., pp. 227–28.

19. Entry for April 4, 1945, in Uchida Hyakken, *Tōkyō shōjin*, pp. 104–5.

20. Entry for May 26, 1945, in ibid., pp. 158–59.

21. Entry for May 27, 1945, in ibid., p. 171.

22. Entry for May 18, 1945, in ibid., p. 149. Hyakken had long suspected that the Bunpō was under the umbrella of the Taisei yokusan kai (Imperial Rule Assistance Association). Its functions were now being carried on by the Cabinet Information Bureau (p. 179).

23. Entry for May 30, 1945, in ibid., p. 174.

24. I have translated whenever possible from the French text reproduced photographically at the head of *Watanabe Kazuo haisen nikki*, but my notes refer to the Japanese translation. Entry for March 11, 1945, in *Watanabe Kazuo haisen nikki*, p. 8. "Mater dolorosa" (Grief-stricken Mother) refers to Mary at the foot of the Cross.

25. Entry for March 12, 1945, in ibid., p. 11.

26. Entry for March 15, 1945, in ibid., p. 13.

27. Miyahara was a specialist in children's literature, especially that of northern Europe.

28. Entry for March 16, 1945, in *Watanabe Kazuo haisen nikki*, p. 15

29. Ibid., pp. 15–16.

30. Entry for March 20, 1945, in ibid., p. 18.

31. Entry for April 3, 1945, in ibid., p. 20. A partial explanation of what happened on Saipan and Iwo Jima is given in the notes to the Japanese translation (p. 21). According to the head of the Joint Army-Navy Information Office, three thousand seriously wounded Japanese soldiers, unable to join the others, committed suicide in the belief that in death their spirits would join their comrades in making the final charge.

32. Entry for May 4, 1945, in ibid., p. 23.

33. Entry for June 1, 1945, in ibid., p. 29.

34. Entry for June 6, 1945, in ibid., p. 30.

35. Entry for June 12, 1945, in ibid., p. 32.

36. Entry for June 20, 1945, in ibid., p. 39.

37. Ibid., pp. 39–40.

38. Ibid., p. 41.

39. Entry for March 10, 1945, in Itō Sei, *Taiheiyō Sensō nikki*, vol. 3, p. 270.

40. Entry for March 15, 1945, in ibid., p. 277.

5. On the Eve

1. Entry for March 13, 1945, in *Takami Jun nikki*, vol. 3, pp. 249–50.

2. Entry for March 17, 1945, in ibid., p. 268.

3. The bowl, known as *Totoya no chawan*, was of Korean origin, used in the tea ceremony.

4. Entry for May 2, 1945, in *Takami Jun nikki*, vol. 4, pp. 4–11.

5. Entry for May 8, 1945, in ibid., p. 36.

6. Entry for May 2, 1945, in Yamada Fūtarō, *Senchūha fusen nikki*, p. 192.

7. Entry for May 11, 1945, in *Takami Jun nikki*, vol. 4, p. 39.

8. Entry for March 21, 1945, in ibid., vol. 3, p. 286.

9. Entry for February 21, 1945, in Yamada, *Senchūha fusen nikki*, p. 83. The Bōsō Peninsula is bounded on the west by Tokyo Bay.

10. Entry for April 18, 1945, in ibid., p. 174.

11. Entry for May 12, 1945, in *Takami Jun nikki*, vol. 4, p. 40.

12. For Tokutomi Sohō's article, see ibid., pp. 55–59.

13. Entry for May 18, 1945, in ibid., p. 53.

14. Entry for July 14, 1945, in *Unno Jūza haisen nikki*, p. 102.

15. Entry for May 28, 1945, in Itō Sei, *Taiheiyō Sensō nikki*, vol. 3, pp. 318–21.

16. Entry for April 8, 1945, in Yamada, *Senchūha fusen nikki*, p. 157.

17. Entry for May 22, 1945, in *Osaragi Jirō haisen nikki*, p. 217.

18. Entry for June 1, 1945, in ibid., pp. 228–32. The *Mariana jihō* was one of several Japanese-language newspapers prepared by the American forces and used for propaganda purposes. See Beigun Manira Shireibu, *Rakkasan nyūsu*.

19. Entry for June 6, 1945, in Yamada, *Senchūha fusen nikki*, p. 282.

20. Beigun Manira Shireibu, *Rakkasan nyūsu*, p. 6.

21. So stated in a postwar survey. It is not possible to say if the respondents to the survey were being truthful. Most of those who believed the leaflets were city dwellers who had suffered a bombing, according to Matsuura Sōzō, *Senjika no genron tōsei*, p. 66.

22. Entry for June 12, 1945, in Yamada, *Senchūha fusen nikki*, p. 289.

23. Entry for March 12, 1945, in *Takami Jun nikki*, vol. 3, p. 240.

24. Entry for May 1, 1945, in *Nagai Kafū nikki*, vol. 7, p. 30.

25. Entry for May 5, 1945, in ibid., p. 31.

26. Entry for July 27, 1945, in ibid., vol. 7, p. 55.

27. Entry for July 31, 1945, in ibid., p. 56.

28. Tanizaki, in his disappointingly prosaic account of the meeting with Kafū in Katsuyama, gives a rather different reason for Kafū's decision to return to Okayama. In Okayama, there was a ration of food every three days, but Kafū was unlikely to obtain any rations in Katsuyama. Tanizaki offered to provide Kafū with a room and firewood, but said he could not accept the responsibility of providing food. See entry for August 14, 1945, in Tanizaki Jun'ichirō, "Sokai nikki," p. 390.

29. Entry for August 14, 1945, in *Nagai Kafū nikki*, vol. 7, pp. 60–61.

30. Entry for August 14, 1945, in Yamada, *Senchūha Fusen nikki*, p. 385.

31. Entry for August 12, 1945, in *Taiheiyō Sensō nikki*, vol. 3, p. 335.

32. Entry for August 11, 1945, in *Osaragi Jirō haisen nikki*, p. 305.

33. Entry for August 9, 1945, in *Unno Jūza haisen nikki*, p. 119.

6. The Jade Voice

1. Entry for March 30, 1945, in Kiyosawa Kiyoshi, *Ankoku nikki*, p. 308. As far back as March 30, 1945, Kiyosawa had heard from a Dōmei reporter that the navy and the army air force favored requesting Russian mediation, but that the army was unequivocally opposed.

2. *Itami Mansaku zenshū*, vol. 2, p. 335.

3. According to the terms of the pact, it remained in effect for one year after either party renounced it. It should therefore have been valid until April 1946, although the Soviet Union denied this.

4. Entry for August 9, 1945, in *Takami Jun nikki*, vol. 4, pp. 370–72.

5. Entry for August 10, 1945, in ibid., p. 377.

6. Ibid., p. 378.

7. Ibid., p. 379.

8. Ibid., pp. 379–80.

9. For a concise discussion in English of the uses of the term *kokutai*, see Ikuhiko Hata, *Hirohito*, pp. 89–90.

10. Entry for August 10, 1945, in *Takami Jun nikki*, vol. 4, p. 396.

11. Entry for August 14, 1945, in ibid., p. 412. The words "the emperor" do not appear in Takami's diary; instead, there are two circles, as if the words had been censored. Evidently, Takami still feared his diary might be read by the police.

12. Ibid., p. 413.

13. Ibid., p. 416.

14. Hata, *Hirohito*, p. 73. He quotes the account of Lieutenant General Yoshizumi Masao, director of the Military Affairs Bureau of the War Ministry.

15. For a detailed account of the last few days before the emperor's broadcast on August 15, see Ōya Sōichi, *Japan's Longest Day*.

16. Entry for August 15, 1945, in Yamada Fūtarō, *Senchūha fusen nikki*, pp. 407–8.

17. Entry for August 15, 1945, in Tokugawa Musei, *Musei sensō nikki shō*, pp. 272–74.

18. Entry for August 15, 1945, quoted in Otabe Yūji, *Nashimoto no Miya Itsuko-hi no nikki*, pp. 309–10. Itsuko's daughter Masako married I Un, the last crown prince of Korea.

19. Entry for August 15, 1945, in Hirabayashi Taiko, "Shūsen nikki," pp. 132–33.

20. Entry for August 15, 1945, in Yamada, *Senchūha fusen nikki*, p. 423.

21. Ibid., p. 427.

22. Ibid., p. 429.

23. Ibid., p. 433.

24. Ibid.

25. Entry for August 16, 1945, in *Osaragi Jirō haisen nikki*, pp. 139–40. More serious plans for a postwar coup d'état are treated in the chapter "Schemes for Survival of the Imperial Line," in Hata, *Hirohito*, pp. 88–159.

26. Entry for August 15, 1945, in Hirabayashi, "Shūsen nikki," p. 133.

27. Entry for August 17, 1945, in *Osaragi Jirō haisen nikki*, p. 312.

28. Entry for August 20, 1945, in ibid., p. 313.

29. Entry for August 15, 1945, in *Takami Jun nikki*, vol. 5, p. 16.

30. Entry for August 21, 1945, in ibid., pp. 56–57.

7. The Days After

1. Entry for August 16, 1945, in Yamada Fūtarō, *Senchūha fusen nikki*, pp. 431–32.

2. Entry for September 3, 1945, in ibid., p. 474.

3. Entry for August 15, 1945, in ibid., p. 430.

4. An article from *Mainichi shinbun* that Takami pasted into his diary listed the names of people who had committed suicide before the Imperial Palace. This was their way of apologizing for having shown insufficient loyalty to the emperor and of expressing the hope that after death they would become gods protecting Japan. Others killed themselves at Atago-yama and near the Meiji Shrine.

5. Entry for August 12, 1945, in *Unno Jūza haisen nikki*, p. 123.

6. Entry for August 17, 1945, in ibid., p. 126. *Taigi* combines emperor-worship with the teachings of the Yellow Dragon branch of Sōtō Zen Buddhism. It was originally in the form of a series of letters by Sugimoto Gorō to his four sons. It was extremely popular among military men, especially young officers, and more than 1.3 million copies were sold.

7. Entry for December 31, 1945, in *Unnō Jūza haisen nikki*, p. 145.

8. Entry for August 27, 1945, in *Takami Jun nikki*, vol. 5, p. 114.

9. Entry for September 12, 1945, in Yamada, *Senchūha fusen nikki*, p. 488.

10. Entry for September 12, 1945, in *Takami Jun nikki*, vol. 5, p. 244.

11. Entry for August 15, 1945, in Yamada, *Senchūha fusen nikki*, p. 432.

12. Entry for August 17, 1945, in *Takami Jun nikki*, vol. 5, p. 17.

13. Entry for August 17, 1945, in Yamada, *Senchūha fusen nikki*, p. 432. There were as yet no American troops in Tokyo.

14. Entry for August 18, 1945, in ibid., p. 434. There were as yet no American troops in Yokohama.

15. Entry for August 27, 1945, in *Takami Jun nikki*, vol. 5, p. 114.

16. Entry for August 21, 1945, in ibid., p. 53.

17. Entry for September 1, 1945, in Yamada, *Senchūha fusen nikki*, p. 457.

18. Ibid., pp. 457–58.

19. Entry for September 16, 1945, in ibid., p. 500.

20. Entry for September 10, 1945, in ibid., p. 485.

21. Entry for September 4, 1945, in ibid., p. 481. Yamada would have said something even more sarcastic if he had known that the *Missouri* was chosen for the ceremony because the ship was named for President Truman's home state.

22. Entry for August 17, 1945, in *Takami Jun nikki*, vol. 5, p. 19.

23. Prince Higashikuni was appointed on August 17, 1945, succeeding Suzuki Kantarō. He was a member of the high nobility (the uncle of Emperor Hirohito). Osaragi Jirō gave an account of an interview by the press with Prince Higashikuni on September 18 at which he was present, in *Osaragi Jirō haisen nikki*, p. 334. Osaragi characterized the questions put to the prince by the reporters as "rather brutal, in the American manner." Prince Higashikuni resigned on October 5, the shortest tenure of any prime minister. He had refused to accede to demands from the Supreme Commander of the Allied Powers for an end to restrictions on political freedom, personal freedom, and religious freedom. For a concise account of the events leading up to the resignation, see Iokibe Makoto, *Senryōki*, pp. 119–21. Iokibe also stresses the mischievous role of the Naimushō (Ministry of Home Affairs) in leaking to the *New York Times* a report that MacArthur and the emperor had met on terms of equality.

24. Entry for August 20, 1945, in Yamada, *Senchūha fusen nikki*, p. 442.

25. Entry for August 20, 1945, in *Takami Jun nikki*, vol. 5, p. 49.

26. Entry for August 21, 1945, in ibid., p. 52.

27. Ibid., pp. 55–56.

28. Entry for August 22, 1945, in ibid., p. 60.

29. Ibid., pp. 60–61.

30. For an account of the oath on ascending the throne, see Donald Keene, *Emperor of Japan*, pp. 139–40.

31. Entry for August 13, 1945, in *Takami Jun nikki*, vol. 5, p. 124.

32. Entry for August 29, 1945, in *Osaragi Jirō haisen nikki*, p. 321.

33. Entry for August 29, 1945, in *Takami Jun nikki*, vol. 5, p. 121. Takami also mentioned that his friend the novelist Kon Hidemi had heard that four thousand

women had responded to the call for one thousand women to serve as "comforters," but this seems to have been a different organization from the one that advertised in the *Tōkyō shinbun*.

34. Entry for August 30, 1945, in ibid., p. 122.
35. Entry for September 8, 1945, in ibid., p. 198.
36. Ibid.
37. Entry for September 4, 1945, in ibid., p. 162.
38. Entry for September 14, 1945, in ibid., p. 261. The Japanese commands are in extremely coarse approximations of Chinese. The second is "You, go over there!" I don't understand the first.
39. Entry for September 21, 1945, in ibid., p. 309.
40. Entry for September 28, 1945, in ibid., pp. 336–38.
41. Entry for September 30, 1945, in ibid., p. 343.
42. Ibid., p. 346.

8. The Revival of Literature

1. For an account of the censorship imposed by MacArthur's headquarters between September 1945 and September 1949, see John W. Dower, *Embracing Defeat*, pp. 406–40. Dower gives "the categories of deletions and suppressions" practiced by the censors (p. 411).
2. Satomura Kinzō (1902–1944), killed in the Philippines, might be considered an exception. His decision to go to the Philippines, although the situation for the Japanese was desperate, probably was an act of suicide.
3. Entry for August 19, 1945, in *Takami Jun nikki*, vol. 5, p. 32.
4. Entry for August 17, 1945, in ibid., p. 18.
5. Entry for August 18, 1945, in ibid., p. 25. In a later part of Takami's summary of the discussion, he said that he and Kawabata Yasunari maintained silence throughout the discussion (p. 27).
6. Ibid., p. 27.
7. Entry for October 13, 1945, in *Nagai Kafū nikki*, vol. 7, p. 80.
8. Entry for September 22, 1945, in ibid., p. 72.
9. Entry for September 9, 1945, in ibid., p. 69. Mention of clouds being swept away recalls the start of the war, when writers rejoiced over the sweeping away of the clouds of Anglo-Saxon culture
10. Entry for September 26, 1945, in ibid., p. 74. In the Tōto Shobō text (which I have followed), this reads: *sakuchō heika bifuku bikō shite Akasaka Reinan sakashita naru beigun no hon'ei ni ma-shi gensui wo towase tamaeri to iu*. The text followed in the Iwanami Shoten and other editions is: *sakuchō tennō heika mōningukōto wo ki jijū sūnin wo shitagae medatanu jidōsha ni te, Akasaka Reinan*

sakashita beigun no hon'ei ni itari Makasa gensui ni kaiken serareshi to iu koto nari. The former text is typical of Kafū's style; the latter is surely a rewriting in simple language.

11. A *mai* was a sheet of manuscript paper with spaces for four hundred characters. Orders for manuscripts even today are made in terms of numbers of *mai*. One *mai* comes to about half a page in English translation.

12. Entry for October 15, 1945, in *Nagai Kafū nikki*, vol. 7, p. 81.

13. In later issues, the proportion of literary essays and fiction in relation to political articles was much increased.

14. Aono Suekichi, "Sensō zakkan," p. 26.

15. Ishikawa Tatsuzō, "Nihon no saiken no tame ni," *Mainichi shinbun*, October 1, 1945. This issue consists of one sheet. Ishikawa's article occupies about half the reverse side of the sheet.

16. *Salomé* was first performed on January 22, 1907, at the Metropolitan Opera, but the second performance did not occur until 1934. Opposition from J. P. Morgan and other powerful backers of the opera to the lurid subject (not suitable to be shown to ladies) had resulted in the cancellation of scheduled performances in 1907. Kafū, in New York at this time, frequently attended the opera.

17. Nagai Kafū, "Amerika no omoide," *Shinsei*, January 1946, p. 28. Maksim Gorky while in America traveled with his mistress. This so shocked the Americans that he was ostracized. He accordingly wrote a stinging attack on the United States and left the country.

18. Nagai Kafū, "Kunshō," trans. Edward Seidensticker, in *Kafū the Scribbler*, pp. 329–35. This was not a new work. Chūō Kōron had been forbidden to publish it in December 1942. Kafū saved it (along with his diary) when his house burned down. See Jay Rubin, *Injurious to Public Morals*, p. 273.

19. The testimony of five writers who agreed that Kafū intended from the start to publish the diaries and for this reason deliberately introduced fictional elements and even changed the personality of the diarist is cited in Ōno Shigeo, *Kafū nikki kenkyū*, p. 5. This undoubtedly is true of *Saiyū nisshi* (*Diary of a Journey to the West*), the diary of his stay in France, but if there is an element of fiction in his wartime diary it is not easy to detect.

20. Ōno gives the variants in the diary for 1945, in *Kafū nikki kenkyū*, pp. 358–67. The text I have used (in *Nagai Kafū nikki*) is fuller than the one published by Iwanami Shoten. It does not refrain from criticizing the Occupation.

21. Entry for May 20, 1946, in Uchida Hyakken, *Hyakkien sengo nikki*, p. 177.

22. *Bunmei* was a literary journal that ran for twelve issues in 1916 and 1917.

23. Entry for January 1, 1946, in *Nagai Kafū nikki*, vol. 7, p. 97.

24. Entry for April 6, 1946, in ibid., p. 112. It is hard to believe that the Americans slaughtered everyone in sight.

25. Entry for May 31, 1946, in ibid., p. 121.
26. Entry for December 31, 1947, in ibid., p. 195.
27. Entry for September 14, 1945, in *Takami Jun nikki*, vol. 5, p. 268.
28. Entry for September 16, 1945, in ibid., pp. 273–74.
29. Entry for September 19, 1945, in ibid., p. 285.
30. Entry for September 21, 1945, in ibid., p. 308.
31. Entry for October 3, 1945, in ibid., p. 363.
32. Entry for September 29, 1945, in ibid., pp. 341–42. It is not clear what the "question" was, but it probably was related to Takami's birth. His mother, who lived in a small town in Fukui Prefecture, was assigned to be the "companion" for one night when the governor of the prefecture visited the town. Takami was born of this night's encounter, and he was depressed throughout his youth by his illegitimacy. When he made his *tenkō*, he blamed his leftist activities on being illegitimate. Takami was the first cousin of Nagai Kafū, who refused to recognize this relationship.
33. Entry for October 5, 1945, in ibid., p. 371.
34. Entry for October 3, 1945, in ibid., p. 358.
35. Takami Jun, *Waga mune no soko no koko ni wa*, in *Takami Jun zenshū*, vol. 3, p. 32.
36. The history of the publication of this work is quite complicated. Takami apparently planned to publish a two-part novel called *Aru tamashii no kokuhaku*. He more or less completed the first part, which was given the separate title *Waga mune no soko no koko ni ha*. The second part, *Kaze fukeba kaze fuku mama* (*Let the Wind Blow as It May*), remained unfinished. Different chapters of the two-part work were published independently in various magazines. The entire surviving text is in *Takami Jun zenshū*, vol. 3.
37. Entry for October 5, 1945, in *Takami Jun nikki*, vol. 5, pp. 371–72.
38. Ibid., p. 374.
39. Entry for October 6, 1945, in bid., p. 379.

9. Rejection of the War

1. Entry for October 23, 1945, in *Takami Jun nikki*, vol. 6, p. 19.
2. Entry for October 22, 1945, in ibid., p. 9.
3. Entry for October 29, 1945, in ibid., p. 63.
4. Entry for September 19, 1945, in Yamada Fūtarō, *Senchūha fusen nikki*, pp. 508–9. Honmoku is a section of Yokohama.
5. Entry for September 20, 1945, in ibid., p. 512. I have not been able to confirm his account.
6. *Kirikomitai* is often translated as "a shock corps," but in this context seems to mean a unit that attacks enemy positions with naked swords.

7. Entry for September 26, 1945, in Yamada, *Senchūha fusen nikki*, p. 531.

8. The *shinchoku*, a prediction that Japan would prosper forever, was pronounced by the Great Goddess Amaterasu on sending her grandson down from Heaven to the world below.

9. Entry for September 20, 1945, in Yamada, *Senchūha fusen nikki*, pp. 513–15.

10. Entry for October 1, 1945, in ibid., pp. 540–41.

11. Ishikawa's article printed that day in the Tokyo edition of the *Mainichi shinbun* has a different title (see chapter 8) and does not contain the hope that General MacArthur would stay in Japan as long as possible. Perhaps Yamada interpreted Ishikawa's plea that the Allied Occupation last as long as necessary as meaning that MacArthur should also remain that length of time.

    Yamada was then living in a part of Japan where the Osaka or Nagoya edition of the *Mainichi shinbun* was more readily available than the Tokyo edition; either may have published a somewhat different version of Ishikawa's article. (I have not been able to consult them.) It is unlikely that Yamada invented the statement.

12. Entry for October 2, 1945, in Yamada, *Senchūha fusen nikki*, p. 542.

13. Quoted in Yoshimoto Takaaki, *Takamura Kōtarō*, pp. 143–44.

14. Takamura Kōtarō, "Shūsen," quoted in ibid., pp. 364–65. This poem is translated as "End of the War," in *The Columbia Anthology of Modern Japanese Literature*, ed. J. Thomas Rimer and Van C. Gessel, vol. 2, p. 431.

15. Takamura, "Wa ga shi wo yomite hito shi ni tsukeri," quoted in Yoshimoto, *Takamura Kōtarō*, p. 147.

16. Entry for October 1, 1945, in Yamada, *Senchūha fusen nikki*, p. 543.

17. The story in question was "A fujin no tegami" (Letters from Mrs. A). See Donald Keene, *Dawn to the West*, vol. 1, p. 967. For the change in guidelines in September 1949 and the ending of the censorship, see John W. Dower, *Embracing Defeat*, pp. 432–33.

18. The account of the case of *Nihon no higeki* is derived from Kyoko Hirano, *Mr. Smith Goes to Tokyo*, pp. 114–45.

19. For an account of the censoring of *The Tale of Genji*, see Jay Rubin, *Injurious to Public Morals*, pp. 258–60.

20. Conversely, some plays long prohibited by the militarists were again performed. *Benten Kozō* was staged in October 1945 at the Daiichi Gekijō in Tokyo. See "Shūsen chokugo gekikai sadan" (Talk Concerning the Theater World Soon After the War), p. 46. *Sakura Sōgo*, which treats a peasant revolt favorably, was staged in November 1945 for the first time in many years. The Nō play *Semimaru*, which could not be performed because of its alleged disrespect toward the imperial family, could now be performed freely.

21. Entry for November 13, 1945, in *Furukawa Roppa Shōwa nikki*, vol. 3, p. 51.

22. Entry for September 22, 1945, in ibid., p. 17.

23. The Japanese controls on films are given in Tadao Sato, *Currents in Japanese Cinema*, p. 101. They not only included a preproduction inspection of all scenarios but forbade such themes as praise for private, as opposed to national, happiness.

24. Entry for November 11, 1945, in *Furukawa Roppa Shōwa nikki*, vol. 3, p. 50.

25. Entry for January 1, 1946, in ibid., p. 81.

26. Entry for February 22, 1946, in ibid., pp. 95–96.

27. Entry for January 19, 1946, in ibid., p. 87.

28. Entry for December 22, 1946, in ibid., p. 177.

29. Manzawa Ryō, "Waikyoku sareta genjō," p. 8.

30. Entry for October 25, 1945, in *Furukawa Roppa Shōwa nikki*, vol. 3, p. 40.

10. Under the Occupation

1. I have translated this excerpt from Cézanne's original letter to Zola, in *Paul Cézanne*, rather than from Takami's version, in entry for November 3, 1945, in *Takami Jun nikki*, vol. 6, p. 94. The italics are Takami's.

2. Entry for November 3, 1945, in *Takami Jun nikki*, vol. 6, pp. 94–95.

3. Entry for November 3, 1945, in ibid., p. 200.

4. Entry for December 21, 1945, in ibid., p. 245.

5. Entry for November 23, 1945, in ibid., p. 208.

6. For a brief description of this film, see Keiko Hirano, *Mr. Smith Goes to Tokyo*, p. 155.

7. Entry for October 23, 1945, in *Takami Jun nikki*, vol. 6, p. 23.

8. Entry for March 13, 1945, in ibid., vol. 3, pp. 249–50. See chapter 5.

9. Entry for October 23, 1945, in ibid., vol. 6, pp. 24–26.

10. Entry for October 24, 1945, in ibid., pp. 26–28.

11. Entry for November 14, 1945, in ibid., pp. 161–62.

12. Entry for March 6, 1946, in ibid., pp. 399–400.

13. Entry for June 18, 1946, in Yamada Fūtarō, *Senchūha yakeato nikki*, pp. 243–44.

14. Entry for February 15, 1946, in ibid., p. 83.

15. Entry for February 4, 1946, in ibid., p. 73.

16. Entry for April 3, 1946, in ibid., p. 147.

17. Entry for August 3, 1946, in ibid., p. 285.

18. Entry for August 15, 1946, in ibid., p. 291.

19. Entry for September 25, 1946, in ibid., p. 318.

20. Entry for October 22, 1946, in ibid., p. 337.

21. Entry for November 30, 1946, in ibid., p. 364.

22. Entry for April 3, 1946 in ibid., p. 146.

23. Entry for February 4, 1946, in ibid., p. 65.

24. Ibid., pp. 65–76.

25. Ibid., p. 76.

26. Entry for March 6, 1946, in ibid., pp. 103–4.

27. Entry for July 12, 1946, in ibid., p. 272. He was planning to make an amalgam of Balzac and Zola.

28. Entry for December 22, 1946, in ibid., p. 385.

29. Ibid.

30. Yamada Fūtarō's *Ato senkai no banmeshi* (*Another Thousand Evening Meals to Come*), a book of essays that originally were published from 1993 to 1997, contains (pp. 220–225) Yamada's harsh appraisal of the Japanese character, as revealed by the publication in newspapers of fictitious victories, like the naval battle off Taiwan. Perhaps, as he became more critical of Japan, he felt less need for vengeance.

31. The problem of freedom was also taken up at this time in popular novels, notably Shishi Bunroku's *Jiyū gakkō* (*School of Freedom*), serialized in the *Asahi shinbun* in 1950.

Anwar, Chairil. *The Complete Poetry and Prose of Chairil Anwar.* Edited and translated by Burton Raffel. Albany: State University of New York Press, 1970.

Aono Suekichi. *Aono Suekichi nikki.* Tokyo: Kawade Shobō, 1964.

——. "Sensō zakkan." *Shinsei,* November 1, 1945.

Ara Masahito. *Daini no seishun; Make inu.* Fuzanbō hyakka bunko. Tokyo: Fuzanbō, 1978.

Ba Maw. *Breakthrough in Burma: Memoirs of a Revolution, 1939–1946.* New Haven, Conn.: Yale University Press, 1968.

Beigun Manira Shireibu. *Rakkasan nyūsu.* Ōsaka: Shinpū Shobō, 2000.

Bix, Herbert P. *Hirohito and the Making of Modern Japan.* New York: Harper-Collins, 2000.

Butow, Robert J. C. *Japan's Decision to Surrender.* Stanford, Calif.: Stanford University Press, 1954.

Cézanne, Paul. *Paul Cézanne: Correspondance, recueillie, annotée et préfacée.* Edited by John Rewald. Paris: Grasset, 1937.

Denoon, Donald, Mark Hudson, Gavan MacCormack, and Tessa Morris-Suzuki, eds. *Multicultural Japan: Paleolithic to Postmodern.* Cambridge: Cambridge University Press, 1996.

Dokusho kurabu, July 1946–November 1947. In *Senryōki shoshi bunken,* vol. 1. Tokyo: Ōzorasha, 1995.

Dower, John W. *Embracing Defeat: Japan in the Wake of World War II.* New York: Norton, 1999.

Duus, Masayo. *The Life of Isamu Noguchi: Journey Without Borders.* Translated by Peter Duus. Princeton, N.J.: Princeton University Press, 2004.

Earhart, David C. "Nagai Kafū's Wartime Diary: The Enormity of Nothing." *Japan Quarterly* 41, no. 4 (1994): 488–505.

Ebii Eiji. "Teikō toshite no chinmoku." In *Kōza Shōwa bungaku shi,* vol. 3. Tokyo: Yūseidō, 1988.

Ei Rokusuke. *Hachigatsu jūgonichi.* Tokyo: Shakai Shisōsha, 1965.

Fukada Yūsuke. *Reimei no seiki: Dai Tōa Kaigi to sono shuyakutachi.* Tokyo: Bungei Shunjū, 1991.

Fukushima Jūrō. *Sengo zasshi hakkutsu: Dai Tōa Kaigi to sono shuyakutachi.* Tokyo: Nihon Editor School, 1972.

Furukawa Roppa. *Furukawa Roppa Shōwa nikki.* 4 vols. Tokyo: Shōbunsha, 2007.

Gerow, Aaron, and Abé Mark Nornes, eds. *In Praise of Film Studies: Essays in Honor of Makino Mamoru.* Victoria, B.C.: Trafford, 2001.

Gordin, Michael D. *Five Days in August: How World War II Became a Nuclear War.* Princeton, N.J.: Princeton University Press, 2007.

Hasegawa, Tsuyoshi, ed. *The End of the Pacific War: Reappraisals.* Stanford, Calif.: Stanford University Press, 2007.

——. *Racing the Enemy: Stalin, Truman, and the Surrender of Japan.* Cambridge, Mass.: Belknap Press of Harvard University Press, 2005.

Hata, Ikuhiko. *Hirohito: The Shōwa Emperor in War and Peace.* Edited by Marius B. Jansen. Folkestone: Global Oriental, 2007.

Hirabayashi Taiko. "Shūsen nikki." In *Hirabayashi Taiko zenshū,* vol. 12. Tokyo: Ushio Shuppan, 1979.

Hirano, Keiko. *Mr. Smith Goes to Tokyo: The Japanese Cinema Under the American Occupation, 1945–1952.* Washington, D.C.: Smithsonian Institution Press, 1992.

——. "Japanese Filmmakers and Responsibility for War: The Case of Itami Mansaku." In *War, Occupation, and Creativity: Japan and East Asia, 1920–1960,* edited by Marlene J. Mayo and J. Thomas Rimer. Honolulu: University of Hawai'i Press, 2001.

Hirano Ken. *Hirano Ken zenshū*. Vol. 13. Tokyo: Shinchōsha, 1975.

——, ed. *Sensō bungaku zenshū*. 7 vols. Tokyo: Mainichi Shinbunsha, 1971.

Hosokawa Morisada. *Hosokawa nikki*. 2 vols. Chūkō bunko. Tokyo: Chūō Kōron Sha, 1979.

Inoue Shirō. *Shōgen, senji bundanshi: Jōhōyoku Bungei Kachōno tsubuyaki*. Tokyo: Ningen no Kagakusha, 1984.

Ishikawa Jun. *Bungaku taigai*. Tokyo: Shōgakukan, 1942.

Itami Mansaku. *Itami Mansaku zenshū*. Vol. 2. Tokyo: Chikuma Shobō, 1961.

Iokibe Makoto. *Senryōki: Shushōtachi no shin Nihon*. Kōdansha gakujutsu bunko. Tokyo: Kōdansha, 2007.

Itō Rei. "Chichi Itō Sei no nikki wo yomu." *Shinchō*, February 1997–March 1998.

Itō Sei. *Itō Sei zenshū*. 24 vols. Tokyo: Shinchōsha, 1983.

——. *Taiheiyō Sensō nikki*. 3 vols. Tokyo: Shinchōsha, 1983.

Jose, Ricardo Trota, ed. *World War II and the Japanese Occupation*. Quezon City: University of the Philippines Press, 2006.

Keene, Donald. *Dawn to the West: Japanese Literature of the Modern Era*. Vol. 1, *Fiction*. New York: Holt, 1984.

——. *Emperor of Japan: Meiji and His World, 1852–1912*. New York: Columbia University Press, 2002.

——. *Landscapes and Portraits: Appreciations of Japanese Culture*. Tokyo: Kōdansha, 1971.

Kiyosawa Kiyoshi. *Ankoku nikki: 1942–1945*. Iwanami bunko. Tokyo: Iwanami Shoten, 1990.

——. *A Diary of Darkness: The Wartime Diary of Kiyosawa Kiyoshi*. Edited by Eugene Soviak. Translated by Eugene Soviak and Kamiyama Tamie. Princeton, N.J.: Princeton University Press, 1999.

Kockum, Keiko. *Itō Sei: Self-Analysis and the Modern Japanese Novel*. Stockholm: Institute of Oriental Languages, Stockholm University, 1994.

Koppes, Clayton R., and Gregory D. Black. *Hollywood Goes to War: How Politics, Profits, and Propaganda Shaped World War II Movies*. Berkeley: University of California Press, 1990.

Laurel, José P. *José P. Laurel: His Excellency José P. Laurel, President of the Second Philippine Republic: Speeches, Messages and Statements, October 14, 1943, to December 19, 1944*. Manila: Lyceum of the Philippines, 1997.

Lebra, Joyce C. *Jungle Alliance: Japan and the Indian National Army*. Singapore: Asia Pacific Press, 1971.

Manzawa Ryō. "Waikyoka sareta genjō." In *Senryōki shoshi bunken*, vol. 1. Tokyo: Ōzorasha, 1995.

Matsumoto Ken'ichi. *Shōwa Tennō densetsu: Tatta hitori no tatakai*. Asahi Bunko. Tokyo: Asahi Shinbunsha, 2006.

Matsuura Sōzō. *Senjika no genron tōsei: Taiken to shiryo.* Kyōto: Shirakawa Shoin, 1975.

Mayo, Marlene J. "To Be or Not to Be: Kabuki and Cultural Politics in Occupied Japan." In *War, Occupation, and Creativity: Japan and East Asia, 1920–1960,* edited by Marlene J. Mayo and J. Thomas Rimer. Honolulu: University of Hawai'i Press, 2001.

Mayo, Marlene J., and J. Thomas Rimer, eds. *War, Occupation, and Creativity: Japan and East Asia, 1920–1960.* Honolulu: University of Hawai'i Press, 2001.

Minami Hiroshi. "Ryūgen higo ni arawareta minshū no teikō ishiki." *Bungaku,* April 1962.

Miwa Kimitada. *Nihon: 1945 no shiten.* Tōkyō: Daigaku, 1985.

Morris-Suzuki, Tessa. "A Descent into the Past: The Frontier in the Construction of Japanese Identity." In *Multicultural Japan: Paleolithic to Postmodern,* edited by Donald Denoon, Mark Hudson, Gavan MacCormack, and Tessa Morris-Suzuki. Cambridge: Cambridge University Press, 1996.

Nagai Hisamitsu. *Chichi Nagai Kafū.* Tokyo: Hakusuisha, 2005.

Nagai Kafū [Nagai Sōkichi]. *Nagai Kafū nikki.* 7 vols. Tokyo: Tōto Shobō, 1958–1959.

Nakajima Kenzō. *Kaisō no sengo bungaku: Haisen kara rokujūnen Anpo made.* Tokyo: Heibonsha, 1979.

Ninagawa Yuzuru. *Haisen chokugo no shukusaijitsu: Kaisō no Matsuo Takashi.* Tokyo: Fujiwara Shoten, 1998.

Noguchi Yonejirō. *Hakkōju ippyakuhen.* Tokyo: Fuzanbō, 1944.

Noro Kuninobu. *Sensō bungaku shiron.* Tokyo: Fuyō Shobō, 2002.

Nosaka Akiyuki. *"Shūsen nikki" wo yomu.* Tokyo: NHK Shuppan, 2005.

Odagiri Susumu. *"Zoku jūnigatsu yōka no kiroku."* *Bungaku,* April 1962.

Ohnuki-Tierney, Emiko. *Kamikaze, Cherry Blossoms, and Nationalism: The Militarization of Aesthetics in Japanese History.* Chicago: University of Chicago Press, 2002.

———. *Kamikaze Diaries: Reflections of Japanese Student Soldiers.* Chicago: University of Chicago Press, 2006.

Okamoto Takuji. "Bungakusha to 'Daitōa Kyōeiken.' " In *Kōza Shōwa bungaku shi,* vol. 3. Tokyo: Yūseidō, 1988.

Ōki Atsuo. *Kamigami no akebono: Dai Tōa Sensō shō shishū.* Tokyo: Jidaisha, 1944.

Ōkubo Fusao. *Shūsengo bundan kenbunki.* Tokyo: Beni Shobō, 2006.

Okumura Kiwao. *Sonnō jōi no kessen.* Tokyo: Ōbunsha, 1943.

Ōno Shigeo. *Kafū nikki kenkyū.* Tokyo: Kasama Shoin, 1976.

Ōoka Shōhei. *Taken Captive: A Japanese POW's Story.* Edited and translated by Wayne P. Lammers. New York: Wiley, 1996. [Translation of *Furyoki*]

Orbaugh, Sharalyn. *Japanese Fiction of the Allied Occupation: Vision, Embodiment, Identity.* Leiden: Brill, 2007.

Osaragi Jirō. *Osaragi Jirō haisen nikki.* Tokyo: Sōshisha, 1995.

Otabe Yūji. *Nashimoto no Miya Itsuko-hi no nikki: Kōzokuhi no mita Meiji Taishō Shōwa.* Tokyo: Shōgakukan, 1991.

Ōya Sōichi. *Japan's Longest Day.* Compiled by the Pacific War Research Society. Tokyo: Kodansha International, 1968.

Ozaki Hotsuki. "Daitōa bungakusha taikai ni tsuite." *Bungaku,* May 1961.

Rabson, Steve. *Righteous Cause or Tragic Folly: Changing Views of War in Modern Japanese Poetry.* Ann Arbor: Center for Japanese Studies, University of Michigan, 1998.

Richie, Donald. *Japanese Cinema: Film Style and National Character.* Garden City, N.Y.: Doubleday, 1971.

Rimer, J. Thomas, and Van C. Gessel, eds. *The Columbia Anthology of Modern Japanese Literature.* Vol. 1, *From Restoration to Occupation, 1868–1945.* New York: Columbia University Press, 2005.

——, eds. *The Columbia Anthology of Modern Japanese Literature.* Vol. 2, *From 1945 to the Present.* New York: Columbia University Press, 2007.

Rosenfield, David M. *Unhappy Soldier: Hino Ashihei and Japanese World War II Literature.* Lanham, Md.: Lexington Books, 2002.

Rubin, Jay. *Injurious to Public Morals: Writers and the Meiji State.* Seattle: University of Washington Press, 1984.

Sakuramoto Tomio. *Nihon Bungaku Hōkokukai: Dai Tōa Sensō ka no bungakushatachi.* Tokyo: Aoki Shoten, 1995.

Sandler, Mark. *The Confusion Era: Art and Culture of Japan During the Allied Occupation, 1945–1952.* Washington, D.C.: Arthur M. Sackler Gallery, Smithsonian Institution, in association with University of Washington Press, 1997.

Sasaki Kiichi. "Sensō bungaku no joseizō." *Bungaku,* December 1961.

Satō Kenryō. *Dai Tōa Sensō Kaikoroku.* Tokyo: Tokuma, 1966.

Satō Masaru, ed. *Sengo bungaku.* Shinpojiumu Nihon bungaku. Tokyo: Gakuseisha, 1977.

Satō, Tadao. *Currents in Japanese Cinema: Essays.* Translated by Gregory Barrett. Tokyo: Kōdansha International, 1987.

Seidensticker, Edward. *Kafū the Scribbler: The Life and Writings of Nagai Kafū, 1879–1959.* Stanford, Calif.: Stanford University Press, 1965.

Shimizu Akira. *Sensō to eiga: Senjichū to senryōka no Nihon eigashi.* Tokyo: Shakai Shisō Sha, 1994.

"Shūsen chokugo gekikai sadan." *Engekikai,* October–November 1945.

Sugimura Masaru. *Nikki ni miru Taiheiyō Sensō.* Tokyo: Bungeisha, 2005.

Sugino Yōkichi. *Aru hihyōka no shōzō: Hirano Ken no "Senchū, sengo."* Tokyo: Bensei Shuppan, 2003.

Suzuki Junji. "Bungakusha no Hachigatsu jūgonichi." In *Kōza Shōwa bungaku shi*, vol. 3. Tokyo: Yūseidō, 1988.

Takami Jun. *Takami Jun nikki.* 8 vols. Tokyo: Keisō Shobō, 1964–1965.

——. *Takami Jun zenshū.* 21 vols. Tokyo: Keisō Shobō, 1970–1977.

Takamura Kōtarō. *Takamura Kōtarō zenshū.* 22 vols. Tokyo: Chikuma Shobō, 1994–1998.

Takasaki Ryūji. "*Ichioku tokkō*" *wo aotta zasshitachi: Bungei shunjū, Gendai, Fujin kurabu, Shufu no tomo.* Tokyo: Daisan Bunmei Sha, 1984.

——. *Senjika bungaku no shūhen.* Nagoya: Fūbaisha, 1981.

Tamaki Kenji. *(Dokyumento) senryō no aki 1945.* Tokyo: Fujiwara Shoten, 2005.

Tanizaki Jun'ichirō. "Sokai nikki." In *Tanizaki Jun'ichirō zenshū*, vol. 16. Tokyo: Chūō Kōron Sha, 1976.

Tokugawa Musei. *Musei sensō nikki shō.* Chūkō bunko. Tokyo: Chūō Kōron Sha, 2001.

Tokutomi Sohō. *Tokutomi Sohō shūsengo nikki: Ganso yume monogatari.* Tokyo: Kōdansha, 2006.

Tōkyō Shinbun Shakaibu. *Ano Sensō wo tsutaetai.* Tokyo: Iwanami, 2006.

Uchida Hyakken. *Hyakkien sengo nikki.* Chikuma bunko. Tokyo: Chikuma Shobō, 2004.

——. *Tōkyō shōjin.* Chūko bunko. Tokyo: Chūō Kōron Sha, 1978.

Unno Jūza. *Unno Jūza haisen nikki.* Chūkō bunko. Tokyo: Chūō Kōron Sha, 2005.

Watanabe Kazuo. *Watanabe Kazuo haisen nikki.* Tokyo: Hakubundō, 1995.

Yamada Fūtarō. *Ato senkai no banmeshi.* Tokyo: Asahi Shinbunsha, 1997.

——. *Senchūha fusen nikki.* Tokyo: Kōdansha, 2002.

——. *Senchūha yakeato nikki: Shōwa 21-nen.* Tokyo: Shōgakukan, 2002.

Yamamoto Taketoshi. *Senryōki bunka wo hiraku: Zasshi no shoso.* Tokyo: Waseda Daigaku, 2006.

Yamashita, Samuel Hideo. *Leaves from an Autumn of Emergencies: Selections from the Wartime Diaries of Ordinary Japanese.* Honolulu: University of Hawai'i Press, 2005.

Yokomitsu Riichi. *Teihon Yokomitsu Riichi zenshu.* Vol. 14. Tokyo: Kawade Shobō, 1982.

Yomiuri Shinbun Sensō Sekinin Kenshō Iinkai. *Kenshō sensō sekinin.* 2 vols. Tokyo: Chūō Kōron Sha, 2006.

Yoneda Toshiaki. "Ichi gunkoku shugisha to tanka." *Bungaku*, May 1961.

Yoshida Ken'ichi. "Henshū kōki." *Hihyō*, January 1942.

——. "Henshū kōki." *Hihyō*, December 1942.

Yoshimoto Takaaki. *Takamura Kōtarō.* Tokyo: Shunjūsha, 1965.

前述如く、「闇市場」はもとは戸別に売を。何故、そこへ「闇市場」が自づと形成されて行く。思ふに、明治初年の頃、戸別に、研食器（食堂）が三軒ある。それから違ひない。食堂の前の、食事処になる

紅列が出来た。その紅列拍手ん、切を売る闇屋が、明草

生づ現れた。また、研倉善を売る闇屋が、前からある

細長した。とんど、経験正作へ学、前からある

（だが）研食善食堂中心

として（前述の食堂する如。）そこ、二軒。

生まれる。C）人だかりが、形成す。

そこ紅を。小さな業主づるが、富り処だ

何用一商品の、再びお高まる。）、富り処だ

とんど、習一品といふが、人だ紅うみるやる成る。

紅食善の人を拍手ん。初め、豊るるのだ。だんだん一般の富

習ひ手が現れる。富り手が、現れる。